ON THE INTERPRETATION AND USE OF THE BIBLE

With Reflections on Experience

RONALD S. WALLACE

SCOTTISH ACADEMIC PRESS
EDINBURGH

WILLIAM B. EERDMANS PUBLISHING COMPANY
GRAND RAPIDS, MICHIGAN

First published 1999

Published jointly
in the U.K. by
Scottish Academic Press
22 Hanover Street
Edinburgh EH2 2EP
and in the United States by
Wm. B. Eerdmans Publishing Co.
255 Jefferson Ave. SE
Grand Rapids, Michigan

Printed in the United States of America

03 02 01 00 99   5 4 3 2 1

*

British Library Cataloguing-in-Publication Data

A catalogue record for this book
is available from the British Library
Scottish Academic Press ISBN 0 7073 0775 9

Eerdmans ISBN 0-8028-4719-6

CONTENTS

Contents

The unfolding of your Words gives light

Psalm 119 verse 130

FOREWORD

A few years ago I was fortunate to be invited to teach for two successive winters at the Discipleship Training Centre in Singapore, and it was suggested that one of my subjects might be '*Biblical Interpretation*'. I could not have found anywhere a more encouraging, dedicated and intelligent group of students. Yet when it came to the selection and preparation of what I had to teach I found myself in difficulty. I knew that after nearly thirty years in Parish work, followed by ample opportunity for further study, lecturing in a Seminary, I should have plenty to say. I regret, however, that I did not seem to be able, in the time at my disposal, to put everything in the order that satisfied me, with the clarity I wished to achieve. Moreover, I could find no text book which gave me the guidance I felt I needed.

The class, however, were very appreciative and responsive. Ashamed at what I had given them I promised to try to write in a little book what was in my mind, and to send a copy to each of them. They promised to pray for me as I tried to do it. I have managed to keep in touch with most of them, engaged now all over Asia in giving their Christian witness — and this is the book! I have to apologise to them that, in order to give it a possible circulation within the wider academic community I have had superficially to clutter the book up with references to my sources of information. If they will simply skim all these away, I am sure they will find its basic structure to be simple, and the things I say to be clear.

I found myself as I prepared it referring, more than I had expected, to my own experience. I found myself doing this, not because I felt that there were aspects of my life significantly worth recording in print, but because I could in this way best and most easily express what I wanted to say on the aspect of the subject before me and, after all, teaching a small class can be a pastoral occasion. I make no claim whatever that my experience should be taken as having any authority.

I must explain that I have not had the ability to visit libraries in order to bring the references fully up to the academic standards which I have hitherto set myself. I write at home, and depend mainly on notes which are at times inadequate.

I am most grateful to my brother-in-law, Rev. R. B. W. Walker, for the enormous help he has given me as I have written this book. He has typed the whole of it straight from my often obscure and sometimes indecipherable handwriting, and shown unfailing patience in the re-doing much that I have re-written and re-arranged — at the same time making the whole of the typescript ready for the actual printer in an even more expert manner than any book I have previously entrusted to a professional.

Dr. Douglas Grant my publisher has been as helpful and encouraging as I have always found him.

I greatly appreciate that Dr. Brian Hardman, the dean of the D.T.C in Singapore was willing to risk having me assist him when, introducing myself to him by mail, I warned him that I had passed my 80th year. The warm friendship of his home meant much to me there.

Edinburgh, March 1999

CHAPTER 1

AN INTRODUCTION TO THE BIBLE

From the time I was a child the Christian tradition in which I was brought up inclined me to regard the Bible as a book apart from all others, and of supreme importance. Its very appearance — the special black covers, gilt edged pages and the title 'Holy Bible' impressed me. On my occasional visit to a Church the congregation stood while it was brought in, laid on the pulpit ledge, and opened with reverence at the place where it was to be read.

I came gradually to know some of its contents. Our daily school 'prayers' consisted almost entirely of long readings, selected mostly from the earlier Old Testament history books (though the Gospels and Acts were not entirely neglected). I heard the same stories read by our Rector repeatedly, continuously and without explanation year after year for thirteen years, and thus became familiar with what happened to Abraham, Isaac and Jacob, to Israel in Egypt and in the wilderness under Moses, to Jephthah, Gideon, Samson, Samuel, Saul and David. Our deputy head-master, whenever he had to take prayers usually read from Isaiah 40 or the whole of Isaiah 55 or the latter half of Deuteronomy 10, and I knew these passages by heart. It was through boys' clubs and camps that my mind was focused on the life and teaching of Jesus, and I became familiar especially with the Sermon on the Mount. Such passages as 1 Corinthians 13, and Philippians 4:4–9 were so frequently read when we had prayers, that I knew them by heart. When it was my turn to take prayers, influenced by what I had heard at an Anglican service, I read from Psalm 139 and prayed also in the words of Psalm 51.

I have no doubt that all this prepared for, and led up to, what happened at a student movement conference, though the event was quite sudden and unlooked for. I have to describe it as an experience of both 'hearing' and 'seeing' (Matt. 13:16) — I cannot tell which was the more significant aspect of it. I heard the text, 'God was in Christ, reconciling the world to himself, not imputing their trespasses unto them' (2 Cor. 5:19). As I heard it, I saw what it pointed to. My mind was focused for the first time in my life upon the Cross. I had read about it, and I had heard some talk of why it happened and what it meant. I had even quite recently written an essay for the philosophy class at the university, comparing the deaths of Socrates and Jesus. But there and then I saw it, and saw that it had the significance the text gave to it. Here was God himself come so that I might be able to find him and know him — in the forgiving love offered to the whole world through the suffering of this man! I realised that the truth not only about God, but about the world, about life, and about myself too, was enclosed in the message which had come to me.

I knew I was on the verge of something quite new and truly wonderful in the way of thought, life and experience too. At first, my mind was taken up entirely with the wonder and importance of what I had heard and seen. Here was a great new world within the Bible inviting exploration! I did not therefore during those earliest days think fully about the personal significance of what I had gone through. It was only after some time that I began to realise that something quite critical had happened to myself. Though I had been very suspicious of the 'evangelical' brand of current Christianity which seemed to make people 'pious', and which laid stress on 'conversion' or being 'born again', I had to admit, and I did so then with quite certain assurance, that I myself had not only 'seen' and believed but had actually passed from death to life and had entered the Kingdom of God.

I knew that I had been challenged, and forced to surrender. The reason why I had not before this seen the light was that I had been resisting it. I began to hear with new force the words of the text I have heard so often and beautifully read at our school prayers, but had too readily applied to others. "'Let the wicked forsake his way, and the unrighteous man his thoughts....For my thoughts are not your thoughts, neither are your ways my ways', saith the Lord" (Isa. 55:7–8).

That it was the hearing of a text from the Bible that was instrumental in the re-orientation of my life continued to be at that time (as it still is) of immense significance. I had always felt that the level of life on which I had managed to live, and its quality too, depended on the thought world to which I had opened my mind — especially the world of religious thought and life. For a year or two I had sought in poetry and in the literature especially of the mystically slanted religions, what would give me satisfaction in this direction. I was now beginning to discover that this whole world of religious thought and inspiration was being radically called in question, especially those aspects of it in which I had taken most pride. Had I not put an entirely false value on these former sources of wisdom and inspiration in which I had tried to find life? Had I not been too concerned with self-development and fulfilment when I should have been constrained to self-denial? I was being forced also to admit that my way of life, too, springing out of such dominant motivation, was as worthless in God's sight as my religious and moral attitude.

It was in the Bible that I now found the new world to which I must now give my mind. I was convinced that it pointed meaningfully to the new direction which my life must now take, and offered what was most worth seeking. The key to what I had now to think and do lay in listening to what it had to say, and in looking to where it pointed, even though its thoughts and ways seemed at times so different from those to which I had accustomed myself. It took over my mind with great power. I had no difficulty in memorising much of it, and knowing where I could find again the multitude of passages, stories and texts that encouraged me on my way, kindled my wonder and imagination, and helped my understanding of the truth and of myself. It gave me the language through which I could most meaningfully and freely express my newly found gratitude and devotion to Christ. I found in it the language through which God had especially chosen to speak to me. Since it was a text from Paul which had initially meant so much to me, at first I concentrated on the New Testament epistles for I had never before even heard what they said about Christ's death and resurrection. But I was drawn on and on into the whole of it.

I had no difficulty in grasping its unity. Even when I turned from the New Testament to read in the Old about Abraham or Jacob, David or the Prophets and their oracles, what came home to me was that I had already encountered in the Cross, the same living, holy and powerful God as they spoke about and put their trust in. I myself seemed to have entered that same world in which they themselves thought and moved. And the Word which they continually heard, and passed on though their witness, accused me of the same failings and sins as plagued them and continued to bring me the same healing and forgiveness as they had enjoyed.

Family tradition already had some influence in my attitude and way of life. We have a genealogical tree going back three centuries and occasionally stories of who was who, and who did what, helped me to understand my 'roots'. The Bible gave me alongside this an even more important new past. Here also I found, told in fascinating and searching detail, story after story of my kith and kin in the great new family of God into which I had now been adopted through Christ my brother (Gal 3:29). Strangely I felt close to them.

CHAPTER 2

DEVELOPING PRESUPPOSITIONS

A Gradual Progress

My progress in theological thinking can be compared with that of the blind man to whom Jesus only gradually and in stages gave the ability to see 'everything clearly' as he learned to look 'intently' (Mark 8:22–26). It took me many years before I was able to view with clear evangelical understanding the relation of one aspect to another of what the Bible brought before me in its presentation of the manifold truth of the Gospel. On quite a number of important theological issues, there had to be much studying, praying, listening, (and talking too!), before I could say with any confidence, 'I see'. As the sub-title of this book suggests, it was my experience with the Bible that both raised these questions in my mind, and helped me to think them out. This was especially the case in my thought about the Bible itself. It took me some time to discover what it was all about, why and how it came into being, how I was meant to approach, interpret and use it.

As text after text brought before me new aspects of God's will and work for the world and myself, I have continually been given new insights which have led to a gradually deepening and fuller appreciation of the revelation of himself and his ways which God is seeking to give us through the book. Looking back I can distinguish three successive stages at which my thought became freshly occupied with one particular aspect of this whole development. I discuss the whole under the three listed headings — Inspiration, Revelation and Salvation history. Though my thought on inspiration proved to be of less decisive importance in determining my theological thinking than the other two, I begin with this subject because it was the first to occupy my mind.

5

Inspiration

It was when I began to experience that the Bible was speaking to me as no other book had ever done, and my mind was being opened both to believe and understand its witness, that I became convinced that the writing of it must have been, in some way, inspired. I can find no better illustration or description of the nature of this experience than that given by Calvin, describing his own case. He called it 'a conviction that requires no reason', and a feeling that can be born only of heavenly revelation. It brought the 'utter certainty' that 'the scripture has flowed from the very mouth of God by the ministry of men' (Inst. 1:7:5).

As to the nature of this 'inspiration', it never occurred to me that I could take seriously the view suggested by some Greek theologians that the minds of the Biblical writers were made entirely passive and that they were used simply as tape recorders for a dictated message. Yet I had also difficulty with the view commonly accepted at our theological college. It was firmly held at that time that the authors of the Bible were simply men of outstanding religious genius and full of wisdom. They were given a unique personal insight both into the mind and nature of God and the human situation. They were then left to deduce and clothe their message in words of their own choosing. I felt I had to take more seriously the prophetic writers own accounts of how the 'Word of God came' to them.

They seemed to be speaking out of a quite unusual and close encounter with the living God himself. The message often came as an unexpected intrusion into their minds. They seemed to retain their own thoughts while other thoughts were given to them. They could never by themselves, even had they been wholly sanctified by God, have either conceived or expressed it. At times it broke in as impossibly good news which they could hardly themselves believe. At times, as it came, they were deeply perplexed, and feared the suffering and misunderstanding in which its delivery would involve them. They had to struggle and keep their own thoughts in control. They were often certain that the very words they received were God-given. That they were able to hear and understand what was said, and were made willing to pass on the message, was a work of the Spirit of God within them, and beyond analysis. I regarded their experiences under the Word of God as unique as their situation was unique, yet I felt justified in regarding them as time and again hearing the 'voice' of God in a way analogous to our own hearing of the 'voice' of Christ at times within our own Christian experience. The frequently used introduction to their oracles, 'Thus saith the Lord', seems at least to imply the hearing somehow of a message which had to be spoken or passed on in the form in which it was given.[1]

The way in which the Biblical text continued to impress itself upon my mind helped to confirm my belief in this direction. Again and again I found that its great affirmations about God, the Gospel and life, its promises, commands and warnings, resounded in my mind as if God himself was speaking them. Through no other literature, however religious, sublime or profound had any such word ever reached and found me in this way. Even though the words were reaching me, as I knew, in translated form, I felt that even the translation faithfully made, retained some of the divine sanction of an original utterance. When I thought over the meaning and the message of what I had heard, I did, of course abstract, and work with ideas and thoughts from the texts, but always I found the actual texts themselves so pregnant with meaning that I had to return again to them, and let them speak. In making use of them I found myself at least paying meaningful lip-service to their having been verbally inspired. When I preached I was never fully satisfied with putting across 'topics' or ideas or 'doctrines' drawn from the text, but I felt I had on occasion to resound the actual text itself or phrases extracted from it in their original integrity so that my hearers could hear them as I believed I had heard them. In my attempts to give counsel or comfort to people, or lead them as I hoped to faith in Christ, I often resorted to the quotation of texts, hoping and praying that my

---

[1] The Psalmists and Job spoke of hearing the 'words' of his 'mouth' or 'lips' (Ps. 17:4, Job 23:12). The Apostle Paul also referred to the Old Testament as containing the 'oracles of God' (Rom. 3:2) and expected his own 'words' to be received as if they had the same kind of origin.

friends through hearing them might see what I had seen and hear what I myself had heard — a hearing that had often come through my own devotional reading of the Word or within fellowship around the Scripture.

Obviously there are many parts of Scripture quite casually written and making no claim to having originated under divine inspiration. It would be ridiculous to suggest that the information, 'Ashur father of Tekoah had two wives', should be held as of the same kind of inspiration as I have ascribed to 'I am the Lord your God'. We need not find the presence of such obviously uninspired passages to raise any serious doubts about the direct inspiration of other parts of Scripture. The Bible is given to us by God not simply as a book of oracles, but also as the account of a long-drawn-out 'salvation history'. When we come across many of the details of this history in the text, all that we need require of them is that they should be reliable.[2] The text can fulfil such a criterion adequately without necessarily involving any claim to have been inerrant. Yet because these 'historical' parts of Scripture have no oracular impact upon us, this does not mean that the more obviously inspired parts of Scripture need not register themselves upon us as we have already described. God has joined these two distinct parts of Scripture closely together so that we cannot define lines between them, and has made each part dependent on all its parts.

It will soon become evident in the following discussion on the doctrine of revelation that my belief that the Scripture was inspired in this way by God inclined me to accept without question the authority of its statements on the central doctrines of the faith which I found at the heart of the whole witness of the Bible. Indeed on such matters I was prepared to agree with many of my contemporaries that the Bible was not only an inspired but an infallible witness. I never felt, however, impelled in any way to extend such authority to the information it ventures as it records its history or as it advances its scientific theories.

Thought about the doctrine of inspiration has come gradually to take a place of lesser importance than it once had

---

[2]   For an explanation of 'Salvation History' see pp. 13–15, and of 'reliability' see pp. 119ff.

in my view of the Bible and indeed in the discussion of any aspect of theology. I have no doubt that I made progress when, as I will go on to show, the attention of my mind was drawn away from the nature of the inspired book to the significance of its witness to Christ and Salvation history. After all, what the Bible points to, and is instrumental in effecting, is much more important than the Bible itself. Yet I have continued to hold much the same view of its inspiration as I had when I first studied it. I can well understand the affirmation of James Denney that 'belief in the inspiration of the Holy Scripture is neither the beginning of the Christian life, nor the foundation of Christian theology; it is the last conclusion — a conclusion which becomes everyday more sure — to which experience of the truth of Scripture leads'.[3] The chief reason why I have bound myself closely and consistently to the text of Holy Scripture is that through it alone I find I am given access to Christ himself as well as to his Gospel. I do not doubt the testimony of those I know to be sincere Christians that they can find Christ present to them in ways and through means beyond the range of my own experience, and I am thankful for all those occasions when I myself have been given marvellous signs of his close and careful providential care. But if I wished to speak with any certainty of how he is to be sought and found today I would have to speak of how he presents himself, to use a phrase of Calvin, 'clothed in his Gospel'. My experience of him is word experience. When he speaks, I find it almost invariably through Scripture that he speaks.[4]

Revelation

Varied thoughts enter our minds when we think of what this word stands for in theological usage. My dictionary defines it

---

[3]   In his late work: *The Atonement and the Modern Mind*, p.9.

[4]   Luther puts it in an intimately personal way in his comments on John 14:1, "If I am a Christian and hold to him, I always know that he is talking to me, and here and elsewhere I learn that all His words are intended to comfort me.' And on John 14:6, 'make sure that these words are embedded in your consciousness, so deeply that you can feel Christ's presence.' Luther, *Works A E* Vol. 24 pp. 13 & 42.

as 'a manifestation of divine will or truth' and there are those who would accept the definition of it as 'the body of truths about God, life and salvation which are given their expression in Scripture'. The lectures in Biblical theology which I heard as a student encouraged me at first to think of it as the complex of religious and moral ideas which one could abstract from the most inspired and progressive parts of the Old Testament which finally found their perfect expression and embodiment in Jesus who laid his life down on the Cross to establish them as the final truth. I was also inclined to accept the view that with perceptive and dedicated minds we could also discover from creation around us a 'natural' or 'general' revelation which would lead us towards the 'special' revelation which we could discover only from the Bible.

As time passed, however, I began to discover, especially from my study of the Old Testament that when God uttered his Word it was not primarily to make the inspired and ready-made statements about himself and the world, which had too much occupied my mind. His chief purpose was, rather immediately to bring about events, and in the long run to create a history. I began to study the book, not for the ideas and doctrines I could cull from its statements about God and life, but rather for its witness to what was happening. I discovered that, as John Goldingay puts it, 'The true locus of God's revelation to Israel is in the events of her history, not in the Bible itself.' The Bible is here to tell us how Israel, 'through the continual intrusion of God's Word into its history",[5] became and continued to

---

[5]   Von Rad. It is important to note how everywhere in Scripture God's word brings about what it declares (Ps. 33:9), enters history so that what he wills in speaking it takes place (Isa. 55:!0–11), sometimes in immediately ensuing events (e.g. Gen. 12:4, cf. Ezek. 12:25), sometimes only after months or years (1 Kings 11:29–39, 12:15). His word can contain promises or threats, that he will 'watch over' for many generations before he performs it (cf. Jer. 1: 11–12). It becomes even more clear in the New Testament that what Jesus commanded, happened — he spoke and the sick were healed, the lepers cleansed and the dead were raised. The Apostles preached and their word was 'the power of God for salvation' (Rom. 1:16).

remain through the centuries the people of God. It reveals
how this purpose was finally fulfilled in Jesus and his Church.
While we are certainly meant to profit from the direct doctrinal
teaching given in so many places in the Old Testament, we are
also meant to read it as the story of how God gradually 'formed
this people of Israel for himself' (Isa. 43:21) so that they would
develop an outlook and a way of life different from those of all
other people. It took centuries of loving creative discipline
under his Word, and its providential control of every aspect of
their lives for this to happen. Yet God gradually wove mercy
and judgment together in all his dealings with them so that
finally their Messiah could be born. In the New Testament,
the same Word as was always active in creating this history
'became flesh and dwelt among us'.

Through the whole series of events of which we have been
speaking, God's purpose has always been gradually to show us
the kind of person he was. Each event was intended to bear
the stamp of his nature. I found Ezekiel especially helpful at
this point in his repeated insistence that God saved the people
of Israel, not only for their own sakes but for the sake of his
holy name. 'It is not for your sake, O house of Israel, that I am
about to act, but for the sake of my holy name which you have
profaned among the nations. I will sanctify my great name'
(Ezek. 36:22; cf. 20:8,11,22,44; Isa. 48.9; Ps. 106:8). The reply
given to Moses, when at the burning bush he asked God his
name, can be convincingly translated, 'I will be whom I will
be' (Ex. 3:14). Moses' chief concern in his question was to
know what God was like. The reply given to it was an affirmation
that he would learn the kind of person God was from the kind
of things he was going to do for him and his people. 'If you
watch and understand what you see you will begin to know
who I am'. The future reference in this translation we have
chosen of this affirmation of the divine name does not refer
only to the final events of the New Testament. Every aspect of
Israel's history can be understood as a declaration of his name.
He declared his unfailing generosity in the blessings and gifts
he showered upon them in their need, his omnipotence when,
having been crushed by ruthless enemies, he marvellously
delivered them, his righteousness when he strictly punished
disobedience. It was especially in the way he held on to them

in face of their own continuous wilful rejection of his leadership and kindness (even when the best of them completely failed him — Isa. 63:5) that the fullest .revelation of who he was became enacted.

Of course as he brought about all these events God had to ensure that their message would be understood. At times he made those whom he was involving in the events well aware of what he was doing to them and with them. More often he gave his explanation to one of the prophets whom he raised up to take a prominent part in Israel's history. They were his witnesses, chosen and trusted individuals to whom he drew especially close. He spoke to them personally and gave them deep insight into what was taking place before their eyes, so that they at least could tell their contemporaries what it all meant and write it down so that its place in the whole history might in due time be fully understood.[6] And it is due to their continuing witness today through their writings that we ourselves have a key to understanding what God was saying as event followed event.

Of course, in the midst of his witness to what he was doing, God speaks of himself quite directly at times in the Bible, and we are as dependent on such self-utterances for understanding him as we are on the history. God's intercourse with the prophets and others could indeed become so intimate and deeply personal and self-revealing on the part of God himself that he could speak of them as being his friends. When he spoke to some of the prophets he shared with them not merely his thoughts and purposes but also his feelings and sufferings. In the case of such prophets as Moses (Ex. 32:7–19), Hosea (Hos. 1–3) and Jeremiah (Jer. 20:7–18) we find him actually putting them through a faint measure of the kind of suffering

---

[6]   Elijah, e.g., claims to have been well informed beforehand of what God was going to do and say when his word brought famine to Israel (1 Kings 17:1ff). Jeremiah claimed that the prophets 'stood on the counsel of the Lord' (Jer: 23:18–22). Amos claimed that the Lord did nothing without revealing his secret to a prophet (Amos 3:7 — cf. Jacob, *Theology of the Old Testament* pp. 190–191).

he himself felt so that they could speak about him later (cf. Ex. 34:6–7, Hos. 11:8–9, Jer. 31:31–34) with all the deeper sympathy. When we want to understand God's revelation of himself in the Old Testament thought we have indeed to pay as much heed to the statements made about God and by God, as to the history that reveals him.[7]

Yet God could never have declared his name adequately by speaking mere words, however clearly and eloquently strung together or by illustrating what he said by heavenly visions. Doing so through history alone could begin to bring out clearly the self-sacrificial cost of his remaining, always in face of Israel's rejection of him, their righteous, wise, merciful and long-suffering God. It is indeed only by looking back from what was brought to light in the Cross that we can understand fully what God was telling Israel about himself all through their history. As G. Lampe says, 'It is in the light of this decisive event' that 'the pattern of God's dealings with his people could for the first time be clearly discerned'.[8] Here is how the history of Israel is meant to be read. Here is God's pure self-revelation. Here is the event that is clearly a Word, and a Word that is clearly an event.

A Salvation History

The history of Israel, as we have it in the Old Testament, can certainly be read as if it were simply the history of one particular nation among many others, mostly larger and more important than itself, such as Greece or Egypt or Rome, all caught up and bound up similarly within the one great movement of universal history. It is not however fully understood if it is thought of as such and discussed in this way. It is meant to be read as if it was ordained by God and set in motion to be, throughout the centuries, a quite unique and distinct stream of history moving within universal history. Here even in the

---

[7] James Packer insists that 'the thought of God as revealed in his actions is secondary, and depends for its validity on the presupposition of verbal revelation (ISBE art. on *Revelation*).

[8] G. Lampe, *Typology* p. 24)

Old Testament there is the beginning of a destined new age for mankind, an age later called the 'Kingdom of God'. It is to be thought of as a history kept in motion and guided to its God-ordained goal by the constantly intruding divine Word (Von Rad).[9] It is to be understood not simply as a history of revelation but as a history of salvation. It was set in motion not simply to reveal the character and nature of God, but to fulfil the saving purpose of his reconciling love, to bring about the redemption of all mankind from the sin, corruption and death under the judgment to which we have brought ourselves by our alienation from God. In choosing the best way to bring about this salvation he has not concentrated his energy on an attempt to mould and control universal history. He has chosen rather to bring about the universal salvation of mankind by working within and through what is to happen as this one nation fulfils its destiny. Having begun with Abraham this history pursues its course through progressive stages, during the rise and fall of many other nations and empires, 'to its God-ordained goal in Jesus Christ' (Von Rad). It was set to find its climax in his life, death and resurrection ('according to the Scriptures' 1 Cor. 15:3–4). It then begins to manifest its universality as it moves on through the centuries of the Church to bring about the consummation of all things (cf. Matt. 19:28) when he returns in power and glory.

We are made continually aware in the Bible of course, that God is also working out his purposes within the general history of all nations. Certainly in the midst of the chaos that seems to prevail within universal history God at times gives clear signs to our faith that he is keeping it within his sovereign and providential care[10] and he so shapes it that he can teach us important lessons. He controls it enough, as Barth points out, to enable Calvin confidently to quote the classical adage,

---

[9]   We will discuss in the chapter on Typology how within this salvation history one event not only follows another under the direction of God but actually prophecies another.

[10]   Time and again in the Bible, pagan emperors, quite unconscious of what God is doing follow the directions of his will, e.g., Pharaoh, Cyrus, Nebuchadnezzar (Jer. 25:9, 27:6).

'History is life's teacher'.[11] 'If the history of fallen man', says E. Rust, 'is generally one of frustration and meaninglessness, the events of salvation history, while occurring within it also transform and redirect it,[12] though in a hidden way'.

Many New Testament passages make us aware, too, that if we are united to Christ we are at the same time being oriented towards and caught up in the powerful forward thrust of this salvation history as it moves all things towards the consummation of all history in the age to come of which we have been speaking. The author of the Epistle to the Hebrews (6:4,5) takes it for granted that if we have 'tasted the goodness of the Word of God' and 'shared the Holy Spirit' we must have at the same time experienced 'the heavenly gift' and 'the powers of the age to come'. John 15 reminds us that if we 'dwell' in Christ and allow him to 'dwell' in us, cultivating a deep personal bond of friendship with him, we will find ourselves inevitably caught up into the works that he is doing as he controls the developing history of the world. Moreover, Paul urges us to think of ourselves as now in Christ belonging to a new family of God of which our membership gives us a new past history. We are no longer 'alienated from the commonwealth of Israel, and strangers to the covenants of promise', but are even here and now 'fellow citizens with the saints and members of the household of God' (Eph. 2:12,19). He explains elsewhere that in Christ we have become 'the offspring of Abraham' (Gal. 3:29), and in the Epistle to the Romans, using

[11] Comm. on Rom. 4:23 and preface to Comm. on Acts — see Karl Barth, *The Teaching of Calvin*, p. xxv.

[12] *Salvation History* p.28. We ourselves believe that the effect which the onward thrust of salvation history has on universal history is outlined by Jesus in the parables which describe the influence which the Word of the Kingdom of God has on the society into which it is introduced. The parable of the *Leaven* describes it as having first a disturbing but then a powerfully humanizing and stabilizing influence on society. The parable of the *Wheat and the Weeds* describes how it can sometimes eventually provoke a vicious reaction from the 'enemy' of all good which can appear for a while even to triumph, though ultimately to be exposed and judged (cf. my *Many Things in Parables*, pp 22–25, 27–35).

another metaphor, he asks us to regard ourselves as having been cut out of what is by nature a 'wild olive tree', and by God's kindness 'grafted' into the 'rich root' of the new olive tree which he has laboured throughout the whole of Israel's history to produce finally in Christ.

These considerations are brought before us in the New Testament so that we can work out for ourselves their practical implications. Since we have a new past, our life need no longer become dominated, as it has been by what is naturally behind us. We have become 'ransomed from the futile ways inherited from our ancestors' (1 Pet. 1:8). Therefore we can break with the old habits and ways, taking no more part in what is unfruitful (cf. Rom. 13:12; Eph. 5:11). And we can become more open to our new future allowing ourselves to become more and more caught up in the forward thrust of the salvation history that is still being worked out in Christ.

CHAPTER 3

FACING THE BIBLE AS A WHOLE (I)

The Unity of the Old and New Testaments

The Preparation for the New Testament in the Old

The New Testament continually makes the claim that the coming of Christ and the chief events of his ministry were foretold in the Old Testament. Jesus was born as he was, and where he was, to fulfil the Scriptures (Luke 1:31–33), and he is spoken of as doing many of the things he did because it was written of him that he would do them (Luke 12:31; 24:44). That he was 'despised and rejected', 'wounded for our transgressions', 'bore the sin of many', is prophesied in Isaiah 53, and Psalm 22 seems to describe in detail many of the circumstances of his death. Throughout this book we will have occasion to discuss more fully the extent and nature of such written prophecies and to hint at how they may have arisen.

If we are adequately to appreciate how he was being prepared for in the Old Testament, however, we must trace how from the time of Abraham, God shaped the social, national and religious traditions within the life of his people Israel. He kept them apart from other nations, seeking persistently with patience, love and ruthless discipline, to mould their customs, thoughts and future ideals. Therefore when Christ came he found not only guidance about his career from the Scriptures, but a place where he could be received as an infant, grow with the favour of God upon him and become 'strong and filled with wisdom' (Luke 2:40). Only through centuries of such training in family life could there have been a home in Nazareth where the Son of God, born as one of ourselves could begin to learn the filial and godly obedience which was to come to its climax in the offering which he made for us, as man, on the Cross. We must not overlook God's miraculous and long-sustained work amongst Israel's womanhood, which came to its climax in Mary of Nazareth. She was wholly devoted to a life in the service of God. Her 'Magnificat' shows how fully her mind had been stored with Biblical lore (Luke 1:46–55), and when the announcement of her pregnancy was made it had become almost second nature for her to say, 'Here I am, the servant of the Lord; let it be with me according to your word' (Luke 1:38).[1] The disciples whom Jesus had to have around him when he began his ministry in Galilee were prepared for their place in his mission with no less care than was his home. The most influential of them had come powerfully under the influence of the teaching and leadership of John the Baptist who had been raised up to point Jesus out to Israel as their Messiah, and to stage his dramatic and deeply symbolic inauguration at his baptism in the Jordan.

There are indeed many other ways in which we could attempt to show the way in which the Old Testament is designed to produce the New. It can be claimed that only through development in Old Testament culture and worship alone could there also have developed the precise thought-forms and fine word meanings that were to enable Jesus and his followers to have at their disposal the language that was necessary if the mystery of what he was to accomplish through his death on the Cross was to be adequately understood.[2] Moreover it is through the analogies derived from the political and religious set-up within Israel's developing history that the New Testament

---

[1]   I am not an expert in the social customs of the other nations around Israel, but I hazard the suggestion that within Israel uniquely the importance of virginity before marriage was stressed (cf. Gen. 34:7 & 2 Sam. 13:12 — 'such things are not done *in Israel*), and that such a special instinct was cultivated in order to ensure that later on one such as Mary would be there for her task in God's purpose.

[2]   'Israel's language articulates an understanding of human existence and the world', which 'for all its dependent relationship and cross connections and analogies to the cultus of the surrounding nations is unmistakably different'. A. H. J. Gunneweg, Understanding the Old Testament, pp. 224–5.

is able to picture for us so meaningfully how Jesus in saving us acts as our Prophet, Priest and King, re-directs our lives, atones for our sins, and takes us under his protection and care.

The Old Testament thus creates the 'tradition in which Christ was born', and gives us the setting in which his life-work has to be understood. We indicate this when we call him by the name of 'Christ'.

The New as Present in the Old

Within the history of the Church, and in the experience of individual Christians today, the slow and unspectacular influence of God's grace can be punctuated by moments of great certainty and clarity (sometimes called 'revival' or 'renewal'). As God was moulding the history of Israel and shaping its thought and tradition there arose occasions in which, more powerfully than at other times, he forced himself into the consciousness of those with whom he was working. The 'divine will to fellowship' (Eichrodt) seemed to break through all normal restraint, and the prophets, or other chosen individuals, sometimes with those around them, were able to speak of themselves as seeing the 'glory of God' or 'the heavens opened', as they listened to what they knew as his 'voice'. Such experiences of liberation, fellowship and responsibility before God are classed by scholars under the title 'theophany'. We believe that such memorable experiences were not confined to those dramatic and critical moments in the affairs of the nation or to the lives of important leaders, but were also open to the ordinary pious believing people of Israel. All members of the community were indeed encouraged ardently to hope for such to happen when they took their sacrifices to the temple at Jerusalem, especially during the great feasts, and sought God's forgiveness and blessing. Weiser reminds us that when the Psalmists encourage the people to hope to see 'the face of God' or to come 'into his presence'[3] they have in mind the quite frequent occurrence of such theophanies to ordinary individuals perhaps quite privately but with no less effective

[3]   In his commentary on the Psalms.

consequences in the lives of worshippers who experienced them.[4]

There is a deep similarity which the Church has always recognised, between the religious experiences out of which the Psalmists speak as they seek to express themselves before God adequately and sincerely on their occasions of prayer and worship in Old Testament times, and the various thoughts, moods and desires with which we feel ourselves possessed as in Christ today we seek self-expression before God. Most Christian people throughout the ages have found themselves unable to coin any better language than the Psalmists lend to them when they sing before the Lord with joy and exultation, or turn to him with true contrition and repentance, or cling to him with desolation and despair. 'Israel', as Muilenburg says, 'has given us words to speak in the presence of the Holy One. They defy the barriers of time and place, and become the interior possession of all who would say what is deepest in the heart to say'. We are convinced that the Psalms can defy such 'barriers of time and space' in this way because when they were composed Christ was present to those who gave them utterance. He was present not as a distant object of vision, but as the source and life of the salvation history in which they were then involved. We find ourselves forced to conclude that to a quite significant extent they themselves were conscious of his real presence at the heart of their experience and worship.[5]

All these considerations encourage us to give due weight to the affirmations made in the New Testament itself that Christ himself was present in Israel (John 8:30–59; Heb. 11:24–28), offering his leadership and strength to the people of God in

---

[4]   Cf. Von Rad, *Old Testament Theology* I:260. 'Jahweh's turning towards her was not exhausted in historical deeds, and in the gracious guidance of individual lives........Here (in the cult) Jahweh was in reach of Israel's gratitude. Here Israel was granted fellowship with him in the sacred meal (cf. Exod. 24). Above all, Israel could be reached by his will for forgiveness!' Cf. also H. H. Rowley, *Worship in Ancient Israel*, p.40: 'The sacrifices were meaningful to a degree far beyond a figurative and merely declarative symbolism.'

[5]   Cf. My *Calvin's Doctrine of the Word and Sacrament*, pp. 27–34.

the wilderness (2 Cor: 3:17–18), sustaining Moses when he needed the strength to endure (Heb 12:24–28). Jesus felt justified in claiming to have been there, personally and deeply involved whenever in Old Testament times the people of Jerusalem rejected the pleadings of a prophet to return to sanity and righteousness (e.g. Matt. 23:37).

G. Ernest Wright points out that the early Christian Fathers 'grasped the Bible's essential unity intuitively in the light of the risen Christ'.[6] They treated the Old Testament as a Christian book, and found Christ continually referred to and intruding into the history. Irenaeus even suggested the thought, which I found later in my study of Calvin, that in his manifestation of himself to the prophets he was habituating himself to enter bodily into humanity. It was a refreshing and illuminating discovery when, early in my ministry as I was preparing to preach on the patriarchs, that I found A. B. Davidson's illuminating interpretation of the visit of the angel to Abraham's tent. 'Rather is the event to be held literal. An angel entered Abraham's tent. He let his feet be washed: the same who in after days washed his disciples' feet. He allowed meat to be set before him; as in after times he asked "Children, have you any meat?" As man he wrestled with Jacob; and now man for ever he wrestles with us all in love; though we oppose him in earnest'.

We are not therefore doing justice to the Old Testament when we think of its Christ as being merely 'prepared for'. or simply pictured from afar in some shadowy form.[7] Even in the midst of the preparation for him at every stage, he was himself always there at the heart of Israel's life. 'The New Testament',

---

6   *Biblical Authority for Today,* p.226.
7   Cf. Emil Brunner, *Reason and Revelation,* p.93. Brunner insists that in this matter 'word and event are still separate. The name still points to a person .... but he is not personally present'. The OT witnesses to Christ 'mainly in a hidden indirect shadowy manner', pp. 134–5. Cf. also James Barr, *Old and New in Interpretation, p.133* and J. K. S. Reid, *The Authority of Scripture,* p.256

says Cullmann, 'completes a process already in effect'.[8] Of course our New Testament experience far surpasses the best that the Old could offer. "Blessed are your eyes, for they see, and your ears, for they hear', said Jesus, 'for I tell you many prophets and righteous people longed to see what you see and did not see it and to hear what you hear and did not hear it (Matt. 13:16).

He indeed comes to make all things new. Yet the 'all things' were all there, faint and frail at times in their expression, waiting for him to lay hold of them and bring them to perfection. H .R. Mackintosh. seeking to make the comparison between Old and New affirms that they had a sense of forgiveness which though more liable to give way before personal calamity was nevertheless 'real and profound'. As Donald G. Miller says, 'Beyond all the limitations of time and space they are all there in Christ. He is there and they are in Him as we are in Him'.[9]

The Miracle of Progress

If we are to begin to appreciate to any full extent the work and wisdom of God described in the Old Testament we must try to review his work as a unity as it is laid before us in its whole range from the time Abraham was called out of Ur of the Chaldees till the birth of Christ. We find two aspects of it especially remarkable and we content ourselves here by touching briefly on both.

We first of all review the way he persistently worked over the centuries within Israel's life to bring about the radical change he sought in the religious morale and outlook of Israel as a people, working with individuals, families, social and other

---

[8]   Cf. A B. Davidson, Theology *of the Old Testament,* p.6. 'The Kingdom of God in its perfect form does not lie in knowledge, but in the life that knowledge awakes .... It could be prepared for only by bringing in, and that in ever fuller tides the life of which it consists. The knowledge of that kingdom could be learned only by men within that kingdom.'

[9]   H. R. Mackintosh, *The Christian Experience of Forgiveness,* p.77. Donald Miller, *Scottish Journal of Theology,* 11:4, pp. 401–2. See Brevard Childs, *Biblical Theology in Crisis,* p.111

institutions, elevating their thoughts, habits and ideals, creating good and wise social customs, developing just laws, awakening concern for the weak and needy in the midst, developing a healthy hatred of the sensuality and idolatry which he himself found abhorrent, inspiring trust in himself and in his fatherly care for each individual. As Wheeler Robinson once said: 'The supreme miracle in the Old Testament is the historical development of the religion of Israel'.

We are meant to notice the quiet and wise strategy through which he persisted unwaveringly from century to century to bring about such change. His way of working is well described in the memorable verses in Isaiah 55 where his word sent from heaven is shown to become absorbed and put to use unobtrusively on earth in the same sure way as seed and rain, quietly sown and gently sent from heaven finally bring the expected harvest. In every generation as he plans the way ahead he chooses to rely on certain individual leaders whom he brings under his transforming personal influence and calls to give themselves to his service. He quietly wins their trust, works with them and trains them to obey him. When he knows that he has won them to himself he makes them quietly and powerfully influential to others around them within the community who open their minds to their teaching. They find themselves gradually supported in their mission by an elect group of people to which God gives an influence far beyond their numbers and status. He protects them and establishes them in the stand they have to take against what is pagan and degrading in their social life. It was in this way that gradually and surely it came about that under God's providential care every movement of opposition to his will suffered confusion, frustration and ultimate defeat.

God also now and then exercised his influence in more spectacular ways. There were important turning points in public affairs when dramatic decisions seemed to be taken by the nation as a whole. We can think of the covenant made at Sinai between God and the people led by Moses (Exod. 24), or the re-dedication of the whole nation after Joshua's great oration (Joshua 24), or of the great day at Carmel (1 Kings 17). That such great turning points in the nation's life occurred, was, however, simply the manifestation of what had already been taking effect in the underground movement of the nation's life.[10]

Another of the remarkable features of the history of Israel is to be found in the way the nation was kept continually looking forward to a great future. In the literature of the great empires to which it was contemporary, we find that they all reached a point when they began to feel themselves in decline and to boost their pride and morale they began to look back to greater days in their past history. In contrast 'any one who studies the historical development of the Old Testament', writes Eichrodt,[11] 'finds that throughout there is a purposeful movement which forces itself upon the attention ... at times static ... but the forward drive breaks through once more reaching out to a higher form of life .... making what has gone before inadequate .... This movement does not come to rest till the manifestation of Christ.' 'The people of Israel', remarks A. B. Davidson, 'were always conscious that as a people of God they were moving on to great things, in spite of failures, and when great things happen they speak of themselves as moving on to greater things'.[12]

Again we have to note that it was only because of the continually intruding Word of God that this hope was inspired and kept alive in Israel. The Book of Ecclesiastes proves that in temperament the men and women of Israel were as naturally disposed to cynicism over the progress of mankind as are many of us today. The majority among them, indeed, misinterpreted the great prophecies almost as soon as they were made, to suit their self-centred nationalism and then lapsed into disbelief. Many of the God-fearing élite among them could give way to severe bouts of despair. God had time and again to rekindle dying embers, as he saw to it that this chosen nation never was able to lose sight of its destiny among the nations.[13]

---

[10] Elijah in his prayer for the apparently decisive turn of events, at the same time acknowledged that God had already by the years of quiet, unspectacular work and in answer to prayer 'turned their hearts back'. The 23rd chapter of Joshua speaks of a period of steady, patient, instructive teaching before the dramatic public avowal of national repentance in chapter 24.

[11] *Theology of the Old Testament*, I:26

[12] *Old Testament Theology*, pp. 2–3.

[13] Cf. e.g. Elijah at Horeb, 1 Kings 19; Jer. 20:7–18.

The Cost of Progress

When we think over this miracle, our minds must also dwell on what it cost God to bring it about. It involved him in the first place in the shame of acquiring among the surrounding nations the reputation of being merely the national God of Israel. What happened during the inevitable wars in which, as the God of Israel, he became involved, made matters worse. When Israel came through as victors, they brought his name into further disrepute by cruelly, and often savagely, abusing those now under their power. And when they themselves had to be disciplined by suffering for a while under defeat and humiliation, many of them, disillusioned and embittered, instead of accepting God's discipline, turned against the one who had loved them so much, and accepted into the heart of their nation's life from generation to generation a hatred against his truth and name.[14]

It is in the light of the description of 'the wickedness of mankind' in Gen. 6:5 that we have to understand what God took on when he adopted Israel as his people: 'Every inclination of the thoughts of their hearts was only evil continually'. They could no more naturally have taken to the truth and hope their God was offering them than any other nation. They took to war, to unnatural lust and savage greed. They were inclined to court death and destruction rather than light and life. That there appeared amongst them, now and then, those who allowed their minds and hearts to incline to truth and goodness, and became great prophets and leaders, was itself the work of omnipotent and determined grace alone.

It was inevitable, therefore, as the presence of God's grace was increasingly felt in Israel, that the resistance of those who became obstinately and finally unwilling to respond to God's summons towards salvation, should become more and more

[14] His crucial way of going about the salvation of mankind is still grossly unappreciated by those who fail to appreciate the shame to which he had to submit himself and allow no admiration to enter their minds for this 'bloody and unchristian' God of the Old Testament.

intense, and resentful as their ways were thus judged and threatened by those who had been won over to him by his patience and love.

Progress therefore brought conflict and division within Israel's life. The more successful the forward thrust became, the more bitter and sinister the opposition. Tragically in the midst of this growingly intense conflict it happened at times that those in Israel who had submitted themselves to his power, discipline and service could allow themselves to slip back into the ways and habits from which he had toiled to redeem them. Indeed, even the élite among them, who had become his most trusted friends, could fail to live up to what he had expected of them, and at times their misunderstanding of his will and their false witness could tarnish the reputation of his name which he had too trustingly committed to them. When, like Elijah, they tried mistakenly to force his support by foolish and unworthy prayers, he loyally held on to them. When, like Jehu, they brought disgrace to his name by the way they carried out his will, he even rewarded them for their achievement in his service.[15] He never gave up, and nowhere, even in the New Testament is the marvellous nature of his unfailing grace and patience more clearly revealed than in the way we see him hold on to Israel throughout the Old Testament. It is simply the full depth of that continually borne cost which becomes clear to us in the Cross.

The Old and the New — the Need of Each for the Other

W. Vischer points out that when we confess our faith in him as *Jesus Christ,* we make it clear that our knowledge of Christ arises from the two parts of Holy Scripture: the Old and New Testaments. The Old is *what* Christ is, the New is *who* he is.[16] It follows that we have to take great care in our interpretation of the Old Testament never to isolate it from the New and in our interpretation of the New Testament never to isolate it from the Old. 'Moses and Elias', says Augustine, 'that is, the Law and the Prophets, what avail they unless they converse with

[15] Cf. 2 Kings Ch.1.
[16] See The *Witness to Christ in the Old Testament,* ET Vol. 1, p.7.

the Lord?'[17] Those who gave us the Old Testament, as Geoffrey Lampe says, were working and writing 'not primarily for their own time but as witnesses beforehand to the coming of Christ and his saving work'.[18] Much of the Old Testament's apparent teaching about God has to be corrected by what we find in the New Testament. We have already seen how important it is that we should understand how false impressions of God can be easily taken from the Old Testament narrative if we fail to read it as the story of how God had to humiliate and conceal himself in order finally to reveal what it all meant in the New

The New Testament must be allowed not only to correct the Old when we gather such false impressions. It must also be allowed continually to enhance Old Testament teaching where it falls short of the goal to which it was intended to move. Jesus said of the Old Testament law, 'I have come not to abolish but to fulfil', and he proceeded to give an interpretation of the old commandments that heightened and intensified their moral force. Indeed when we want a true picture of what happens when God's righteous judgment (indeed his 'wrath')[19] are fully expressed we have it, not in the Old Testament but in the New. Paul points out that in Old Testament times God never took sin as seriously as he did when he dealt with it fully and decisively in what came upon Jesus as he exposed himself to it on Calvary. Reviewing the whole Old Testament period his verdict is that God 'passed over' (Rom. 3:25) or overlooked (Acts 17:30) the full seriousness of all sins then committed by humankind and that only in the Cross does he fully declare his righteousness. It is only here and now as we face what has happened in the Cross that we can know the full extent and nature of the enmity against God which has been there behind all the pride, lust and sloth that have too often

---

[17] *Sermons on the New Testament,* ET XXVIII, p. 232:2.

[18] *Scripture and Tradition,* p.29.

[19] This is a point in which Karl Barth is always ready to give his witness. Cf. *Church Dogmatics,* ET II/1 p.395. 'The threats and executions of punishment' in Israel he affirms are certainly not 'indifferent facts', but may give only a 'faint reflection' of the 'infinitely more terrible happenings that took place on Good Friday'.

marred our lives. It is only here that we realise how serious
and urgent is our need for repentance (cf. Acts 17:30–31). It
is important for us to realise that it is only as a preparation for
the New that the Old comes into its own, and is lifted up to the
level which God meant it to occupy in his continuing work as
a source of enlightenment in the Church, of equal importance
to the New.

While we are aware of the need of the Old for the New we
must equally be aware of the need of the New for the Old. It
often happens in Christian circles that attempts are made to
alter the composite picture we are given of Jesus in the Gospels
and to present him otherwise. The "Jesus" I was asked to picture
and follow when I was a youngster was the perfect embodiment
of the greatest ideals which were then hoped for as the solution
of moral problems that were thought to thwart the onward
march which humanity was destined to take on its progress
towards an earthly kingdom of God. The ideals he embodied
in no way arose directly from the development of Old
Testament religion. He was to be regarded, rather, as the
product of the yearning of all nations as humankind evolved
towards the true future God had in store for us. He was
crucified in his own day by a world that was not then evolved
sufficiently to listen to him and we his followers had to struggle
and to be ready to suffer in taking up the cause for which he
died. When I was studying for the ministry one of the most
popular religious books was entitled 'The Christ of the Indian
Road'. One of our leading missionaries from India in a lecture
he gave suggested to us that if we would try to appreciate what
Hinduism really taught and stood for we would find ourselves
with a new basis for a much transformed and truly universal
Christianity. Time and again there has arisen, even within the
Church, a tendency to reject every close connection between
Jesus and Israel as a deceptive distortion of the truth. It began
in the early centuries with Marcion who rejected from the
Canon many parts even of the New Testament that he found a
hindrance to faith because they rooted the New Testament
too deeply in the Old. It fosters the story that Jesus, before the
beginning of his ministry went for a significant time to the
East so that he could embody purer truth in his teaching than
the Jewish faith could give him. It found its most militant

expression during the anti-Semitism which flourished under Hitler and in the Christianity of the German Church which accepted his programme and discouraged the use of the Old Testament in its worship.[20] A tendency more recently obvious has been the unwillingness to accept that the cultic and prophetic traditions of the Old Testament can give us an adequate interpretative background for understanding Jesus' path of suffering. We must therefore take off the old Jewish wrappings and look at the event with less biased eyes.[21]

It is my belief that such attempts to re-present Jesus to the world other than as the Christ of the Old Testament do the whole Gospel a grave injustice. We cannot alter the fact that God himself (and from all eternity) chose the place and time at which the Saviour of the world was to be born, the race to which he was to belong, the exact kind of role he was to fulfil and the form in which he was to be 'lifted up from the earth', both on Calvary and in the continual proclamation of the Church to draw to himself all humankind in every generation, casting out the power of evil from its throne in the life of this world and in all human hearts (John 12:31–33). Everything he did and taught when he entered his life-work was devoted to establish the claim to be the Messiah of the Jews. 'Salvation', he said, 'is from the Jews' (John 4:22).

The Unchanging Value of the Old Testament Text

An equally important aspect of the interdependence of the two parts of the Bible is the need of the New Testament to have its teaching continually illustrated and supplemented by constant reference to the text of the Old. Since there seems to be a failure in current Biblical exposition to use the Old Testament in this way we feel it worth while to give it some particular attention at this point in our discussion.

[20] In 1985 as an understandable reaction against what they regarded as the brutal invasion of their country by Israel I found some of the Elders of the Palestinian Churches there stubbornly resistant to having the Old Testament read in their services.

[21] See R. S. Wallace, *The Living Fountain*, p.35.

It was in a parish deeply affected by the depression and unemployment which followed the first world war that I began to realise the value and importance of taking my text at times from the Old Testament rather than from the New. It was when I studied the current expositions of the prophets then available to me that I was able to discover, talk about and illustrate the tendency of wealth in a society to flow towards those who already have it, about the ease with which the 'haves' are enabled to deprive and oppress the 'have-nots', of the need for the flow of money to be controlled and of the duty of the Church to concern itself about the problems, as the prophets did, in the name of the Lord.

It has been said that there is hardly a Christian virtue that is not better illustrated in the Old Testament than in the New. For a preacher, for instance, who is concerned to reinforce by illustration the New Testament teaching on chastity and its abhorrence of the violation of marriage there is what Luther calls the miracle of Joseph in the house of Potiphar. 'By the singular wisdom of the Holy Spirit this miracle has been set before us as an example to the whole Church. Yes for the whole world. Nothing else like it can be found in the Holy Scriptures.' Where, anywhere else, could there be found a more perfect illustration of Jesus' beatitude, 'Blessed are the peace makers' (Matt. 5:9) than in the Old Testament story of how Abigail stepped into the breach to save David from committing the bloodshed that might have spoiled his whole future? Indeed the close correspondence between the texts (cf. 2 Sam. 32–35) suggests that the story was as much the inspiration of the beatitude as its illustration. The New Testament is very sharp and concise in its many warnings against our being led to destruction by vice, e.g., 'God is not mocked, for you reap whatever you sow!' It can afford to be so eloquently brief because the Old Testament, which is in the mind of its readers, is already full of vivid pictures in story, history and proverb of men and women who have been led into hopeless misery because they have allowed their lives to become dominated by self-will or vicious habit of mind or body.

It is in what it both reveals and illustrates about the long-term working of God's Spirit and providence in the lives of those who believe in him, that the Old Testament most powerfully comes into its own and proves how indispensable it is as part of the whole Word of God. The New Testament describes often and with vivid detail the *beginnings* of the friendship which Christ sets up between himself and those whom he calls into discipleship. It also gives us the assurance that God will hold on to us, even though we fail at times to honour him. Yet, except in the unique case of the Apostle Paul, its short time-span, and the quick change of its focus, prevents us from being able to find out how these particular beginnings develop. It is obvious that for all the important details of how God gradually works things out for good as we follow Christ through our whole span of life we are meant to become dependent on the great number of Old Testament whole-life stories and sketches, and the autobiographical meditations in the Psalms. It is these stories that tell us how God can hold on to us when we in later years tend to forget him or even almost cast him off, of how he can weave both mercy and judgment together in the web of our career, discipline us and even break us down when, and as far as we need such treatment. They tell us how he can keep us in a life of continual renewal and glorious liberty as we surrender to him.

I have been grateful at times in my preaching to be able to show from the story of David how being forgiven (marvellously and freely!) by God can at the same time involve our having at the same time to bear, even at great cost, the earthly consequences of our past, and how much can be at stake in the attitude with which we submit to what now happens to us. How powerful a lesson it can bring to a modern congregation if we trace the career of Judah, to remind them of his utterly shameful early affair with Tamar, of his youthful dislike for Joseph, his implication by consent in his sale to Egypt, of the deceit he then practised on his father, and then ask them to listen to the prayer he made to Joseph for mercy on Benjamin and his old father — the evidence of a completely transformed inner attitude of mind and heart through twenty years of discipline and suffering under the hand of God! (Luther says he would give anything if he could learn to pray to God with the same genuineness and ardour as Judah prayed to Joseph). The many family stories in Genesis can remind us, in an illuminating way, of God's will for us in the difficulties and dangers even of Christian family life as he leads us on today 'through childhood, manhood, age and death' to 'keep us still his own'.

In our evaluation of the Old Testament alongside the New we have to note that the Psalms are the most indispensable part of the whole Bible when we are seeking to find the words we need for everything the New Testament Gospel itself inspires and teaches our hearts and minds to pray for and to pray about. Christians in every age have found themselves more able to 'pour out their hearts to the Lord' by using the language they give us than by seeking to coin expressions and phraseology of their own. 'O my God', writes Augustine, 'how did I cry to thee when I read the Psalms of David, those canticles of faith, those sounds of Godliness which exclude the swelling of the Spirit'.[22] Luther, like Augustine, made much of the fact that Jesus himself prayed them in the language they gave him and that it is his Spirit within us that inspires our praying in the same words today.[23]

At an important point in our communion service the pastor is given to say, 'Beloved in the Lord, draw near to the holy table, and hear the gracious words of the Lord Jesus Christ'. This appeal is followed by selected encouraging invitations and promises from Jesus' own sayings. We ourselves can, if we will, find the Old Testament even more full of such 'comforting words' and enabling us, if we will listen, to encounter him with us today and to hear his voice. We may be indeed greatly impoverishing ourselves and those whom we may have around us to lead in worship, if at this point and in all these matters we have dealt with in this section, we fail to use to the full what the Old Testament offers to us.

[22] *Confessions*, IX: 4,8.
[23] Cf. Augustine, Commentary on Psalm 61.

CHAPTER 4

FACING THE BIBLE AS A WHOLE (II)

The Story-Prelude to the Bible

Prelude and Pre-history

In considering the Bible as a whole we have to reserve a special place in which to discuss the first eleven chapters of Genesis. We have to become aware of the highly important place they are designed to take within it as a whole, and of the tenuous strands which link them up with every part of it. They are much more than a preliminary introduction indicating the nature of its contents and extolling their importance. They are like a prelude to the whole which must be kept in mind as a key to understanding what follows. Like the Prologue to John's Gospel they have to be often referred back to as we go through the whole book. If the will of God is to be done in Israel by those who are chosen to hear his Word and enter his service their basic outlook on life, their expectations of providential help, their understanding of the meaning of what happens around them and to them, must all be radically different from those held among the nations who do not know the God of Israel. These early chapters of the Bible in Genesis were designed by God to be continually held before the mind of the children of Israel to form in them an attitude towards God and the view of life and its purpose, distinct and different from that of any other nation. It is our belief that throughout the whole Old Testament period those who were faithful to God derived through the circulation of the tradition expressed in these stories an outlook on God and life that helped to keep their culture, thought, worship and ethics uniquely distinct, as their history moved towards Christ under the Word of God. It is of course when we come to the New Testament that these early stories come into their own and are now fully able to yield the meaning and message it was always in God's mind for them ultimately to have.

The work that Jesus did for us in saving us is certainly well described when we keep in mind the analogy given to us throughout the whole Old Testament history of him as our Prophet, Priest and King. But, an even greater New Testament insight into what he has done for us and can mean for us today is to be derived from these preliminary chapters. I have in mind, of course, the view of Christ as the second Adam who has come into our midst to face all the same temptations and struggles under which we ourselves are doomed to fail, in order to overcome in our place and for us, so that his victory and perfect life can become ours as we claim it by faith and make it our own. It was when I began to understand this aspect of our salvation that I began also to understand the full implications of our becoming united to him and receiving personally all he seeks to give us through his incarnation and life as well as through his death.

Moreover it is within these preliminary chapters alone within the whole Old Testament that I find myself given any adequate pre-glimpse of how deep and vicious is the mental and spiritual plight from which Christ has come to rescue us.[1] The New Testament acknowledges its deep debt several times to the Cain and Abel story. 'Why did Cain do it?', asks John. He gives the answer he found in the story: Because he 'was of the evil one',

---

[1]   Elsewhere than in these chapters, even when it refers to Satan, the Old Testament does not dwell seriously in any way on his sinister nature or power. It was in the thought and writing of the inter-testamental period that the minds of religious writers began to be occupied, as they are in the New Testament, with the existence of the 'principalities and powers of darkness' headed by the Devil which Christ has to overcome, thus taking with full seriousness what is implied in the early chapters we are discussing. We would regard it as merciful that God hides from us the direct aspect of our plight till he is about to deliver us from it.

and 'he murdered his brother because his own deeds were evil and his brother's righteous' (1 John 3:12). Cain had allowed himself to become wholly possessed by the virulent and murderous hatred that had made the 'evil one' himself rebel against God. But he found himself in his abject position unable to give it any expression when he came before God and felt again under condemnation. He therefore gave vent to all he felt as he turned on his brother, whom he knew God loved, and murdered him instead. It is from this story we can now understand more clearly what happened when our God himself in the person of Jesus now apparently defenceless stood before us blameless and seeking our friendship and, instead, 'we crucified him!' During the shock and shame that were expressed in our newspapers when two small boys were found guilty of murdering another, one of the leading writers for our '*Scotsman*' newspaper observed in a leader, 'The desire to kill and inflict pain is natural and innate'. Paul sees sin so constantly arising from this innate attitude Godwards that he defines it as 'enmity against God' (Rom. 8:7. Cf. Eph. 2:15–16. NRSV has 'hostility'), and we are always meant to remember that it derives much of its power by seeking to work subtly, remaining hidden like the serpent in the early story. It can be destroyed when it is exposed, and one of the important insights in the New Testament drama enacted in the Cross is that in destroying evil and breaking its power for ever, Christ allows it fully to expose itself for what it is. Thus he made a 'public spectacle of the powers of evil as he led them in his triumphal procession' (Col. 2:15, NEB).

One of the many other reasons why these early chapters of Genesis were written was to give us in our minds a very rough idea[2] of the pre-history of humankind before Abraham. They

---

[2] The fact that this prelude to the Holy Book has the form of a history differentiates it radically, we are told by experts, from all the mythical introductions to other contemporary mid-eastern religious literature. These religions all begin with stories of how their gods (and often their goddesses too) were themselves the product of conflict amongst extraneous 'mythical' forces in various forms. For an introduction to the study of this striking contrast see e.g. Sarna, *Understanding Genesis,* pp. 8–11, and Cullmann, *Salvation in History,* pp. 93–94 and 138–144.

have been described as an early *credo* of Israel linking up the God of Israel with the God of all nations, and the history of Israel with the history of mankind. In doing this they to remind us also of the important fact that the humanity God chose to work with and use for his purpose, when his choice settled on Abraham and his descendants, was that of an Adam labouring under the guilt of bondage to an evil power that wills to pervert and destroy what is good, naturally full of unease before the God who has made him, and the helpmeet God has given him as his companion and lover, tending always to spoil the happiness God made him to enjoy, to be suspicious where he should be trusting and to cast blame on the other where he should accept it himself, and tempted sorely in the weakness derived from his folly to be kept in alienation from God by 'the lust of the flesh, the lust of the eyes and the pride of life' (1 John 2:16. Cf. Gen. 3:6).

Wisdom in Story

Even though the contents of these chapters are arranged in the *form* of a history for the good reasons we have mentioned, I myself have never thought of them as intended to give us actual historical information. The important influence they have had on my life and my theology has been due entirely to my interpreting them as just 'story'. During the quite extraordinary week which we had here in Britain after the tragic death of Diana, a correspondent to the *Guardian* newspaper wrote: 'We have a powerful need to make sense of things, to find stories that connect what happens in the world'.[3] A recent writer has given a more theological explanation to the same basic urge. 'Where human knowledge reaches the limit of what can be logically or scientifically explainable, creative imagination steps in to provide order and meaning to the intelligible transcendental realities by speaking in picturing symbols'.

Looking back over my life I believe that this basic need to 'connect' and 'to find meaning' in all the absurd things that

[3]   Judith Williams.

were happening around me in life was met in a very healthy way, during those early days, by the story of Adam and Eve settled by God in the garden, listening to the serpent, betraying God's trust in them and finally condemned to expulsion, shame, decay and death. I cannot remember when and how I came to know the story but it laid hold of my mind quite decisively and was an immensely powerful influence on my whole outlook as a whole and my thought about myself. It has held on to me all my life. I think it was gain to me that I was able to grow up during my adolescent days tending to blame humankind rather than God for the mess and tragedy around me, and taking some of the responsibility on myself. I was indeed thankful for being treated better than I deserved, rather than lapsing into fretfulness about what I lacked. I am glad, too, that it had the effect of making me sensibly restrained in my approach to the opposite sex, of making me feel it was a healthy thing to observe decent convention in dress, and that modesty and chastity were praiseworthy virtues.

I am grateful that I found myself unable to yield to the quite prevalent temptation, even in those days, to feel that life was entirely meaningless. I certainly at times began to toy superficially with other thoughts about life. I remember feeling the impact of the doctrine of pantheistic pre-existence offered in Wordsworth's *Intimations of Immortality* when his poetry began to fascinate me — the idea that my birth meant the temporary imprisonment of a truly divine soul within an unworthy environment for a while. But I am thankful that the story of creation in Eden and '*Paradise Lost*' proved more durable. It was, of course, when I heard the 'Word of the Cross' that I began to realise how merciful it was that I had been prepared quite unknowingly all my life with a thought background that inclined me to accept the Gospel when I heard it. Had I not had it as a child I would not have been as ready to respond to the revelation that finally brought me to faith in Christ.

It has been of great interest to me to find serious theological writers, on a much more sophisticated level than that to which I have ever been able to rise, saying things about the human search for meaning and purpose in life, very similar to those which I much more dimly felt in my childhood. They use the word 'myth' where I have up till now used the word 'story'.

They point to a general feeling prevalent today especially among those who have trained, and sometimes limited, their minds to think 'existentially'. If we are honest, they tell us, we will admit that there is much in life that is meaningless and even threatening. The things they say are reminiscent of those said in the Bible by Job and Ecclesiastes at their worst moments and in their most unguarded moods. A preacher recently expressing his own inner feeling uses the flood story as he believes it was meant to be used to speak to his people of 'an uneasiness within us, to a wearisome feeling that about the edges of the world we experience there lurks a danger — a danger that order and reason may break down, that chaos may break in on us'.[4] He does this, of course, in order finally to help them to rejoice all the more that 'we are on the other side', but he does probe accurately a widespread questioning human feeling. What is behind all this deeply tragic and absurd chaos that seems at times to threaten us and how are we to react to it? Why, if we are to survive, are we continually to 'watch' and be on the alert? It is basically one question — with many sides. Who are we? What have we done? And what are we here for?

Those who have become subject to such feelings about life find that such questions as they are forced to ask can be met only by our being given an insight beyond our reach if we remain dependent on the level of ordinary conceptional thought using the processes and methods of scientific or psychological research. They find that the best hints that can help them to come nearest to understanding themselves and the world around them is by entering a world of myth. — finding stories which somehow express the way they understand themselves in the world! With such an understanding of the word 'myth', I would have no objection to describe these stories in Genesis by using such a word, regarding them not as man-shaped but as God-shaped myths, designed to enable us in the measure of perplexity we have to live as Christians with answers that keep us in touch with himself and his word while we live

---

[4]   D. E. Gowan, *Reclaiming the Old Testament,* p.74

in the midst of our questioning. 'Scripture', said Paul, possibly referring to this aspect of its work, 'is able to make you wise unto salvation' (2 Tim. 3:16, AV).

These same stories are also designed to give us wisdom in the midst of the questioning that must inevitably arise as we face other problems and absurdities presented to us in the created world around us. Obviously the One who is meant to be thought of as the Creator, who in the beginning said, 'Let there be light', is the Lord, the God of Abraham, Isaac and Jacob who had redeemed Israel from Egypt.[5] The story of creation is therefore meant to remind us today that it is the Lord, whom we know because he has redeemed us — Jesus, the Son of God, who came in the flesh! — who was there presiding with the Father over our creation. It is the same purely gracious overflowing love and goodness that we know in our salvation that is behind the creation of the universe and all that is in it. God did not make us because he needed to fill up any felt lack within himself for something to give him an outside interest or a helpful companionship. He is the God who is glorious and blessed in himself for ever. And he desires that man should enjoy something of the blessed community that he has within himself. This is why he makes it possible for humankind in the togetherness of men and women to reflect something of his image, as he shows his tender sympathy and understanding of Adam in his possible loneliness. Moreover he intends that there should be a bond of understanding and sympathy between man and the animal creation. As a sign of this intention, he brings every species of animal before Adam so that they may have their apt names from one who understands their natures. In this context we are told that whatever brings conflict, disturbance, disaster, disease and death into the world was not intended to have any reality or place in his creation. it is an aspect of the absurd intrusion of the evil that will finally be abolished in the coming New Creation.[6]

[5] We accept the view that these chapters took their final form after the redemptive experiences that Israel went through as the people of God.

[6] The Prophets look forward to the cessation of all conflict in the creaturely world (Cf. Isa. 11:9, 65:25),and we have to note Paul's hope that all creation itself will be liberated from bondage (Rom. 8:20–21).

In this connection our attention can be drawn to one feature in the strikingly significant following genealogy of the line of Cain and the line of Seth. It is especially the children of Cain who will suffer most in their banishment from his near presence, and it is on them that he is described as, out of pure grace, lavishing in abundance the secular cultural gifts that we human beings need so much to make our purely secular life not simply bearable but full of comfort and colour. It is the children of Cain that God is described as especially endowing with skills to excel in what we today would call the liberal arts and sciences. Music and craftsmanship — the power to build and make things — are indicated (Gen. 4: 19–22).[7] We are meant to note at the same time that very soon Lamech, the father of those so well-endowed, learned how easy it was to kill another person with one of his clever son's swords, and found pleasure in singing a song, possibly in celebration, accompanied by the music of another of his sons. Even then God had to begin to face the risk and the tragedy that some might use the skills that were his gifts to bring destruction not only to human life but to the present earth itself.

The Movement into Salvation History

Certainly as we come towards the end of these chapters and are introduced to Noah, the Flood and Babel we begin to wonder if we are not on the point of leaving the world of story and entering the realm of events that can be researched and called 'historical'. When I was a student it was impressively told us that here and there around us were to be found remnants of a decadent civilisation covered by a huge layer of

---

[7]   Personally I have found this story yielding also another important implication about how we are meant to evaluate some of the gifts of music and artistic ability when we seek to put them to their use in life for which God has given them to us. The story indicates that they were given to humankind chiefly to be expressed and enjoyed and experienced in our pure secularity (Cf. My *Calvin, Geneva and the Reformation,* pp. 102–104.)

silt, with evidence on the top, of the survival of another better one, and of course even then there were serious people looking for remains of an ark on Mount Ararat. Moreover the historical information yielded from archaeological remains of the period indicates that people, one time in a certain area, did build colossal towers, one of which might be referred to in Genesis XI.

I find myself, however, even at this point, much more deeply impressed by what these incidents tell us if I allow them to speak alongside and in continuity with all the other stories we have just been considering. The story of the Flood certainly gives us the marvellous historical example of the man Noah but I accept the view expressed in the book of Isaiah that its most important feature is the oath God made that he would never again be so unrestrainingly wrathful as he was in the 'moment' he said, 'I will make an end of all flesh' (6:3). He would ensure that there would always be a stable background of history in which he himself could work out his redeeming purpose and those who trusted him could show their trust and love as Noah had done (cf. 9:11–17). In pledge of this he gave the sign of the rainbow, and entered with all mankind the covenant of peace which will 'never be removed' (Cf. Isa. 54: 9–10).

It is in the light of the covenant of mercy and stability for all humankind, and in spite of it, that we are meant to read what happened at Babel. There was nothing wrong in the basic aspiration of men and women to rise towards heaven and to be with God and like God, to come to understand in God's way and with God. God made his human creatures to want to take each other by the hand and say, 'O magnify the Lord with me and let us exalt his name together' (Ps. 34:3). But at Babel it was all to be done in self-oriented pride in independence of God and by self-centred effort.

If the lust and licence that deserved the Flood were hateful to God, the pride and arrogance displayed in the plain of Shinar are even more reminiscent of what brought Adam and Eve to their shame at the beginning. Now it has become obvious that as history is so graciously allowed to evolve there will be no way by which humankind can be brought back to him through its own collective development. Yet God, in response to Babel, restrains his anger and exercises his judgment so as to keep his covenant. No longer will there be such destruction as followed the Flood.. Instead, now he merely limits, separates and scatters. As human pride seeks to express itself in any future collective form there will arise the division, tension and confusion that will destroy all hoped-for progress apart from his grace.

If a covenant of mercy followed the Flood however, the decisive historical move towards the beginning of an entirely new era on earth follows Babel. The eleventh chapter after its tragic beginning continues with a long genealogy that moves us into Salvation history. It moves us towards Abraham and the promise that indeed all nations will be blessed by God in their togetherness. Knowing the whole course of this Salvation history as we do, we interpret this promise correctly when we think of Christ and Pentecost. Here at Pentecost through the transforming Spirit, men and women of all tongues and races begin in true humility to speak together and indeed know themselves drawn together into the true human commonwealth God intended for them. It is achieved through Christ's sacrifice and in his body. It is the result not of a decision suddenly made by God on the ground, as it were, and in the midst of his growing problems. It originates in the purpose of his grace even before the foundation of the world, we are told (1 Peter 1:20, NEB), and it was already announced in the prophecy made to Satan in the presence of the woman confidently and triumphantly at the very moment she fell (Gen. 3:15). In that prophecy, made even there and then, we can trace a hint of the long-drawn-out conflict that is to follow and of the personal suffering of the One who is to overcome.

CHAPTER 5

THE APPROACH TO INTERPRETATION

Two Avenues

'The message of the Bible', says R. Prenter, 'does not itself leap directly from the closed book into the mind of the individual, but comes through a living Church which places the Bible in the pulpit, schoolroom and prayer closet.'

The mention of a 'schoolroom' within this context is a reminder that its interpretation is a task involving dedicated and expert scholarship. It has become accepted, in all modern hermeneutic studies that, if we are adequately to understand the Bible, we must take full account of the human origin of all the texts that make it up. We must therefore, especially in the initial stages of any search for understanding, employ the same kind of skill and scholarship as is put to use in the interpretation of any other corpus of ancient literature such as the poems of Homer or the works of Seneca. How helpful it was at school to have the teacher with his expert knowledge, and a reliable book of notes on the text open before us as we studied English or Latin drama or poetry. So today with the Bible.

There is, however, one unique feature of Holy Scripture which makes it different from any of the books we studied in the schoolroom. We must take into account the frequency of the signature attached to many of its most important oracles: 'Thus says the Lord'. It was in the course of Salvation history, and under the constraint and inspiration of the 'Word of God' that the writers of the Bible toiled at the task God gave them. We ourselves have already made clear our conviction that the same Word of God as originally brought the text of the Old Testament into being was spoken finally, fully and in a unique way in Jesus Christ. It was also continually heard and encountered in the early Apostolic Church by those who participated in its fellowship and worship and were active in its mission as it increased and spread. The inspiration and power of the same Word of God also lay behind the writing of the books of the New Testament.

If we ourselves are to be in a position fully to understand and interpret the meaning of the Biblical texts, we must be continally aware of the importance of this quite unique factor in its occurence. God has therefore opened up for us through our interpretation of Scripture especially at the heart of our Church worship a way of listening for and hearing the same Word of God as originally inspired the Prophets and Apostles. His will is that through our use of and experience with the Bible today we ourselves should continue to encounter the forgiving and renewing power of the same Word of God that lay behind the whole course of salvation history and gave rise to the witness of those who wrote it. It is in the midst of such living encounter in Church worship that God gives us most meaningful light on what the Scriptures meant to those who wrote them, and thus can mean to ourselves today.

The best efforts we can make in our private study and 'schoolroom' can certainly bring much light on the circumstances under which the text was written, the situation of the author, the kind of person he was, and his intentions and feelings. They can mention that a 'Word of God came' and analyse the message it then gave, but they cannot allow us any introduction into the heart of that living and transforming experience which is so necessary if we are fully to appreciate what happened.

It is important that a book on Biblical interpretation should lead the thought of the readers along both these ways that God has opened up to enable the Scriptures to yield the message they are meant to give us today. The usual order of discussion is often first of all to deal with how the Bible is to be interpreted with the help of secular skill by the pastor in the study or the scholar at his desk and in classroom, followed later with a more practical discussion on the use of the Bible in the life of the Church and of its individual members. It is my conviction that today more attention needs to be drawn, and primary concern to be given, to hearing the Word of God from lectern and pulpit within the gathered congregation at worship. We here, therefore reverse the usual order of discussion. Scholarly work itself, moreover, if it is to be fruitful in the study of the Bible, in particular, should be undertaken in faith, with restraint and reverence. The schoolroom should therefore be one within the Church.

A Continuing Footnote

It is important that before and throughout our discussion of this whole subject we should realise that the interpretation of Scripture is at the same time both a gift and a task. This is why we have entitled this section 'A Continuing Footnote'.

Interpretation is certainly a task. We will be reminding ourselves in the forthcoming discussion, not only of the skills we need to put to use, but of all the complex processes involving long and patient study, research, careful planning, ordered worship, sincerity of mind, sense of calling and earnest devotion — all involved in the task.[1] We will also have to keep in mind how infinitely serious is the nature of the responsibility that has been laid on us in being entrusted by God with such a task and how serious can be the consequence of slackness and carelessness. Paul prided himself that he 'worked harder' (1 Cor. 15:10) under the grace of God than anyone around him, and he reminded Timothy that it was those who 'labour in preaching and teaching' especially with persistence who are most worthy of honour (1 Tim. 5:7; 2 Tim. 4:1–5).

We must not forget, however, that the interpretation we are seeking must come to us as a gift, granted to us by the sheer grace of God. 'Those most sadly err', said Luther, 'who presume to understand the Holy Scriptures and the law of God by taking hold of them with their own labour and study'.[2] The verse in 2 Peter 1:19 that the 'prophetic message' is 'as a lamp shining in a dark place' has given rise to the comment that it does not give light after it is understood, but it illumines our

---

[1]   Karl Barth, *Church Dogmatics*, Vol. 1/11, p.713
[2]   W. A., LVII, p.185: quoted by A. Skevington Wood, Luther's *Principles of Biblical Interpretation*, p.13.

understanding. In a self-revealing comment in one of his sermons, Augustine explains how he had been enabled to 'discover by force of meditation and to develop in words' the meaning of a difficult text. Thanks had to be given, he said, 'to him from whom I have sought, from whom I have asked, unto whom I have knocked'.[3] With all our skills and expertise the answer we need most will be given to us only as we are content to wait at the door for God in his grace to open as we knock and to give as we ask. Everything depends on our attitude as we knock, wait and seek.

That in face of Scripture we can still seek in order to find means of course that we can still use our reason and skill in the search for its meaning. Luther discusses this use of reason, and differentiates between two different ways in which we can put it to use.[4] We can use it to intrude our own thoughts upon God's Word or we can use it to subject our thoughts to God's Word. It is to the latter use that we must dedicate our reason. Our main concern must always be to allow the Scriptures to yield their own meaning, to realise that any award for the toil we have expended is given to us by the sheer grace of God.

[3]   *Sermons on the New Testament, XXI 37 ET, p.96.*
[4]   W. A., XLII, p.35: quoted by A. Skevington Wood, *ibid*, p.14.

CHAPTER 6

THE INTERPRETATION OF THE TEXT

(1) Within the Worshipping and Gathered Church

A Shared Responsibility under Christ

When we focus on how the Scriptures are to be interpreted within the Church, we find ourselves having to concentrate first of all on what happens as the pastor preaches the 'Word of God' from the pulpit and the people, listening, seek to hear such a 'Word' through what is being said. The expectation of both pastor and people is that Christ, himself in the midst, has been with the pastor, answering the prayers and guiding the preparation, and that he is with the people themselves to help them to understand as they listen.

We are encouraged to hope for such a presence of Christ himself to preside over the interpretation of the Scriptures by the prolonged incident related in the closing chapters of Luke's Gospel, where he drew near to the two disciples on the road to Emmaus and "interpreted to them the things about himself in all the Scriptures" (24:27) making their hearts, as they later put it, 'burn within us while he was opening the Scriptures to us' (v.32). It was later the same evening that he appeared to the twelve and 'opened their minds to understand' (v.45). This incident in Luke's Gospel is told as if it were a sign and foretaste of an entirely new and significant experience which Jesus intended to repeat again and again within the Church which he was at that time beginning to create. The Apostles could take it as a promise that when they now met together to seek understanding from the Scriptures about the meaning of his life, death and resurrection he would be there 'in the midst' to take control in this intimate way over what they were doing.

47

The authority and leadership of the Apostles in the interpretation of the Scriptures was not questioned in the early Church. Those who heard them preach became convinced that the Word they were listening to was given to them by sheer divine insight and was to be received as the living Word of God himself (1 Thess 2:13), as powerful in its effect as it had been when it was spoken by Jesus himself. Through Peter's first attempt at such exposition of the Scriptures thousands were added to the Church, and as the preaching continued day by day (Acts 2:47), 'the Word of the Lord', grew mightily and prevailed (Acts 19:20).

It is our belief that gradually, as the Apostles passed on and the Church developed, the leading responsibility for the interpretation of Scripture was gradually taken over by those who were regarded as the successors of the Apostles. Their calling and skills were recognised by the Church, and they were trained and ordained to fill the vacant place of the Apostles. The living Christ honoured their unique ministry as he had that of the Apostles themselves. There seems to have developed from early in the Church's life a ministry of the Word — Pastors set apart to devote themselves to the special task of interpreting the Scriptures and tending to the flock. This does not mean that there were not among the laity those who found themselves becoming expert in the understanding of the Word. The New Testament Epistles were obviously written to congregations where many were prepared continually to devote thought and prayer to this task, and there is no doubt that they were vocal about it. The lay members of the New Testament Church were encouraged to 'examine the Scripture for themselves' in order to 'see whether these things were so' (Acts 17:11). No doubt they could expect, even while listening to the pastor, to hear a Word which gave them a different slant on the message of a chosen text. Indeed they had a responsibility to judge and perhaps even correct the preaching. Paul believed that the layman in his day could possess the 'mind of Christ' and 'judge the worth of everything' (1 Cor. 2:15–16).

We believe we are justified therefore in claiming that interpretation of the Scriptures within the Church should be regarded therefore as a ministry shared between pastor and congregation. It is our aim in this chapter to make as clear as possible how this task should be fulfilled by both pastor and people.

The Implications of the Preaching Ministry.

The emphasis given in the New Testament Epistles to teaching and exhortation indicate that preaching within the Church at that time quite often aimed to be no more than the expert exposition of a passage of Scripture. The congregation required to be taught which doctrines to believe or avoid. They needed ethical guidance into the new Christian way of life. They needed to be reminded of the teaching and works of Jesus. Paul no doubt had this kind of didactic and exhortatory preaching in mind when he urged Timothy to present himself to God as 'a worker who has no need to be ashamed, rightly explaining the word of truth' (2 Tim. 2:15). In a similar way a pastor in the work of the pulpit today will find that a large proportion of the effort in preparing and planning the sermon must be devoted simply to such teaching and exhortation. The preparation will often involve hard work on the original texts and on commentaries by scholars. There will be much concern to arrange the material and to put across the message as well and as convincingly as possible. Much of the preaching of Jesus himself can be described simply as 'teaching' — about God and life and himself — in simple language and with telling illustration. He earned himself the name of 'teacher'.

The Scriptures, however, are full of great and thrilling affirmations uttered as if by God himself about his own faithfulness, righteousness and love. They resound at times with invitations to his people to come to him, to trust him and to fear and tremble before him. They contain warnings, commands and commandments to obedience. It is when we are faced with such texts that we realise how inadequate it is to think of our ministry in the pulpit as being simply that of the expositor and teacher, even as the 'interpreter of Scripture'. Their message cannot possibly be uncovered by their being analysed or explained evidently with a didactic aim. To convey such words of God to our people with the full clarity and force with which they were originally meant by God to retain, we have to take seriously the promise given by Christ that he will be in our midst not only to interpret but also to preach what we preach. We have to seek not simply to explain but to re-sound and re-echo these invitations and commands in words adapted to their modern hearers, believing that he himself will be with us to take the words we utter and make them his own, so that our voice will be listened to as if he himself were speaking in our place.[1] We have already noted how Peter in his first Epistle identified the word which was heard in the Church through the preacher and brought new birth to its hearers, with the same eternal and powerful Word of God spoken in all past ages and enduring for ever (1 Pet. 1:24-25; cf. Isa. 55). The implication is that through the preaching of the word of Scripture within the Church today there can be brought about a living encounter with the same Word of God which was heard when the original text was inspired and written. It is Calvin who in his teaching brings this out more emphatically than any other commentator I know. Speaking of what happens in preaching he comments on Isaiah 55:11, 'The Word goes out of the mouth of God in exactly the same way as it goes out of the mouth of men; for God does not speak openly from heaven, but employs men as his instruments.'

There is one further aspect of what preaching can mean to us and bring to us within the Church that it is important to keep in mind. God desires that preaching should become within the Church 'the power of God for salvation' (Rom. 1:16). Our salvation was brought about by the Word of God once for all spoken in history when Jesus was born, lived, died and rose again. God has ordained that the forgiving, renewing and transforming power of that once-for-all event is to be encountered in every succeeding generation of the Church's life as it is proclaimed in the preaching of the Church. We are meant to experience this transforming power at work when what Christ has done is proclaimed before us as we worship in his name. As we hear what happened for us there and then, time seems to vanish and it happens to us here and now. The

---

[1]   Cf. Rev. 1:20, John 10:4,16,27. We can believe, of course, that such a hearing of Christ's voice can and will take place also when the aim of the preacher is simply to teach.

past event can be spoken of as 'made present to us' as it is proclaimed to us. God means us to have the same kind of experience when we celebrate the Lord's Supper in which we 'show forth the Lord's death', this time in symbol and action as well as in word. And if we are fully aware of what God is longing to give us in this celebration, we will not be content with making it the occasion of merely 'remembering' what happened for us, but rather of receiving what is symbolised: 'Christ himself and all his benefits'.

Jesus referred to the powerful effect that the preaching of the Cross was intended to have in our world today when he said, 'Now the ruler of this world will be driven out and I, when I am lifted up from the earth, will draw all people to myself' (John 12:31-32). His being lifted up referred of course to the event of his being crucified (cf. John 3). It also refers to his forthcoming ascension with all power to heaven. It was also his intention that it should refer to the proclamation of his Cross after he was lifted up. In this saying he is making the promise that where the proclamation of the Cross takes place in every age he, the ascended Christ, will be there in power to cast out of the hearts of those who hear, if they will surrender, all the power of evil that holds them in bondage. He will hold them to himself with a drawing power, which will determine their eternal destiny.

Preaching indeed is God's gift given us to make what God has done in Christ a present life-giving and transforming reality within our world today.[2] Through it I not only hear re-told the

---

[2] It is in the explanation given in Exod. 13:3-16 of what was to be understood as happening at each Passover Feast that we are given a hint of how we, too, are to understand what God means to happen, both through the Proclamation of Christ crucified and risen, and in the celebration of the Lord's Supper. In the Passover ritual each participant was urged to regard the past event which had so dominant an influence in the life of their nation as having become, through their participation in the feast, the most dominating present reality in their own lives - the past event was not just 'remembered' but made powerful again in its 're-presentation'. Cf. the Mishna: 'In every generation it is the duty of every man to consider himself as having come out of Egypt.'

Biblical account of what Christ had done but am brought into living contact with the 'reality of Christ himself and the whole mystery of salvation'.[3]

Enlightenment, Pastoral Concern and Care

It becomes obvious at this point in our discussion that as the Gospel is preached with the emphasis that we have just described, the response called for from the congregation will be not only a special kind of 'hearing' but also a special kind of 'seeing'. The preacher will say not only 'hear' the Word of God but also 'look' at what God has done, and pray for insight to be given by the Spirit into its meaning. The concern the pastor will have is well expressed by Paul in his Epistle to the Ephesians. He recalls there how he had laid open to them in his preaching the riches of Christ's 'glorious inheritance among the saints and the immeasurable greatness of his power for us who believe' and his prayer was that they might receive from the Father, 'a spirit of wisdom and revelation' so that with 'the eyes of your heart enlightened you might know what is the hope of your calling' (Eph. 1:17-19).

In a later chapter of this book we will discuss fully the surrender and obedience of mind and will that the Word of God finally demands of us if it is to be heard not in vain. Here we are reminding ourselves of what is simply the first stage of this life-work. Yet it is a crucial aspect of our faith-response to the Gospel. Jesus spoke about it often, and he urged those to whom it had happened, to regard it as a special mark and miracle of God's power and grace. 'Blessed are your eyes for they see, and blessed are your ears for they hear', he said to his disciples. 'Truly I tell you, many prophets and righteous people longed to see what you see, but did not see it, and to hear what you hear and did not hear it' (Matt. 13:16-17).

It cannot by any means be taken for granted that when the Gospel is preached, even with the most demonstrable conviction and power, that those who hear what is said will

---

[3]   Cf. Schillebeeckx: *Sensus Plenior and the Roman Catholic Tradition,* p.133.

respond with conviction and faith. The good news can fall on deaf ears. Jesus lamented time and again that people, having ears would indeed 'listen and never understand, ... indeed look but never perceive' (Matt. 13: 14-15). He referred to, and warned against the hardness of heart that caused such inner abstruseness (Mark 8:18-19) and he grieved that anyone within the hearing of the Word should remain in such a condition. He was continually praying that those around him should become humble enough to receive, by God's grace, the insight to begin to see who he really was so that they could come to him and find rest (Cf. Matt. 11:25-28). It was a result of this continual prayer on behalf of his own committed disciples that finally, after an acutely concerned session of questioning, he was able to elicit from Peter the marvellously fruitful confession of faith in himself as the 'Messiah, the Son of the living God'[4] on which he prophesied that his Church would be founded, and which he was thrilled to recognise immediately as an exceptionally outstanding work of the Father in answer to his prayer (Cf. Matt. 16:16).

The preacher or teacher today who fully understands how much the fruitfulness of the ministry given them depends at times on the 'seeing' of what is pointed to in the proclamation or the lesson will at times share the same desire as Jesus had to enter conversation with those who have been listening to ensure that they have grasped the full reality of what has been presented to them in sermon or lesson. There is no doubt that traditionally, at least in the Reformed Church, one of the purposes of the visitation of the homes of the people by the pastor was so that when it was helpful or necessary what was said in preaching could be followed up by pastoral counselling

---

[4]   Tracing the progress of the disciples in the Gospels it is obvious that the faith derived from insight could grow in clarity and conviction. Peter had obviously previous experiences of inward illumination in the presence of Jesus (Cf. especially Luke 5:1-11). We believe we are justified in taking the growth of sight from confusion to clarity in Jesus' healing of the blind man at Bethsaida as a sign of how he sometimes gives inward sight too, in gradual stages.

where people had possibly missed the full challenge or comfort that were being offered in the Gospel.[5]

More recently, however, within house and lay Bible study groups, and variously organised cell-groups within the Church, I have found people around me becoming much more articulate and open about their faith, and I have found myself personally given more frequent and more fruitful opportunity for meaningful pastoral conversation than was apt to occur during the more routine pastoral visitation, important though such visitation is for many other reasons.

In the early Church where they sought to bear each other's burdens intimately within the fellowship, such pastoral concern was shown, not only by those who were in leadership but more often of each member for another (Cf. Gal. 5:1-2). The hints we have in the book of Acts of the organisation of the Church at Ephesus seem to indicate both a special weekly gathering on the Lord's day and frequent house gatherings in localised cell groups where each could make a more individual contribution and this must have been typical of many other towns. Paul when he said farewell to the elders at Ephesus at the end of his ministry among them could remind them that he had proclaimed his message not only in public but 'from house to house', and of how 'I did not cease day or night to warn everyone with tears' (Cf. Acts 20: 18-20). The uplifting newness of what their faith had brought to those early Christians would inevitably draw them together often so that it could be continually expressed and shared. They found that in order to resist the temptation and meet the antagonism they had now to face from the world around them they had to cling to each other in Christ for the strength they needed.

[5]   A model for such counselling and its effectiveness can be found in 2 Kings 6:15-17. The young servant of the prophet Elisha, who must have listened to many assurances about his safety in the service of God, was nevertheless still a prey to hopeless fear till he was assured by the personally addressed word, 'Fear not', and at the same time prayed with: 'O Lord please open his eyes that he might see'.

Undoubtedly at such house gatherings they would pray for one another and for the world around, sharing their problems and experiences, and inevitably their minds and talk would focus on the Word of God as they sought renewal, encouragement and guidance through such written Scriptures to which they would have access, and prayed together for enlightenment.

Pastoral Intercourse and Interpretation

As within the Pastoral Intercourse we have been discussing, the bond between pastor and people is more and more deeply formed, the interpretation of the Scriptures within the common worship of the Church becomes itself enriched by a pastoral dimension. Christ, on earth, was never content to exercise a ministry that in any way fell short of seeking and reaching the particular individual need of each person around him. At the end of his sermon to the multitude on the mountain he pointedly addresses a personal challenge to each hearer as to the response that had to be made (Matt. 7:24-27). He described himself as the one who was always ready to leave the ninety and nine to go and seek that one which was lost. H. R. Mackintosh pointed out to us in class that 'Jesus best sermons were preached to one person' and warned us once that in delivering sermons we did not really begin to preach until we could look at our people and say, 'You'. Even though there are accounts of his healing 'all who were sick' (Mark 1:32), we need not imagine that there was anything 'wholesale' about the work. The accounts of his method in teaching prove that each was treated with intense interest in every aspect of the need they presented.

Christ's ideal for the Church as he meant it to develop is implied in the picture he gives of it in the 10th chapter of John's Gospel. Viewed as a whole it is the one flock of the one great Shepherd who once for all laid down his life for it. Yet it consists of many such flocks which each reflect the structure and unity of the whole, each one flock having one shepherd. As the one great Shepherd of the sheep is filled with concern and infinite care for the welfare of each flock and each one, so each pastor is to be filled with the same intense care for each and is meant to know each intimately and to be known by each so that he too is inspired to self-sacrifice for each.[6] Such pastoral concern will evidence itself in the preaching of a pastor. It will of course have its effect on the interpretation of a text for it will influence what he or she finds in it. The sermon, moreover, will even at times tend to take the form of conversation with an individual. Citing my own experience I think I allowed this pastoral aspect to develop in my preaching unfortunately too late in my ministry. Not that I did not try to be faithful in visiting my flock as often as possible. In the pulpit, however, I was concerned primarily to be faithful in expounding the text before me as a faithful minister of the Word of God, and in the efficient delivery of the sermon. I think part of the fault lay in the local tradition which I inherited during my early ministry. I had been inclined, by what was too often taught us in our training for the ministry and set before us as an ideal, to overestimate the lasting importance of the oratorically

---

[6]   We recognise that there is and has always taken place within the Church the kind of effective preaching ministry which does not seem either to depend on or give rise to this pastoral intercourse. We think of the great evangelistic crusades, which took place, e.g. in Italy in the eleventh century called the 'great Hallelujah', in Edwardian days under Moody and the remarkable ministry more recently of Billy Graham, where the kind of directly personal pastoral relationship, which we have been describing could not possibly occur between preacher and each particular hearer. We have to acknowledge too that at times within the Church unusually effective and attractive 'preachers' have drawn 'crowds' into their congregation. We realise also that the Gospel is furthered in certain areas by very large congregations meeting under a multiple ministry, the pastoral work being carried out by those who have no responsibility for the preaching. We should be grateful that such ministries and such forms of Church organisation occur and are so manifestly used by God. I believe, however, that we should avoid organising the Church as if such large congregations begin to be thought of as a norm for the future. It is our belief that Jesus, in John, chapter 10, was sketching out an ideal to aim after.

constructed and effectively delivered sermon. To find help I studied various preachers' great sermons and even political speeches. I did not realise that in trying to make myself effective in this way I was actually distancing myself from my people. Yet my style and aim in what I was doing in the pulpit did through time change in a quite radical way. Instead of seeking to move my people as if they were a crowd listening to a speech (and sometimes as I had been doing this there had been not very many there!) I began to feel at times that I wanted to enter dialogue with them each as individuals and I adopted a much more conversational style. I thought of Jesus addressing that thronging crowd around him in Galilee with one chief concern in mind, to seek out and give a special word to one individual: 'Who touched my clothes?' (Mark 5:30). I thought of Augustine's comments: 'Many thronged him, one touched him', and wished it could happen in exactly that way for all of them.

The Ministry and Voice of the Laity

Most preachers become conscious of how much their interpretation of Scripture, and the 'liberty' afforded them in their preaching ministry, can depend on the expectation and receptivity of the people who are there regularly in Church. It is characteristic of the Reformed tradition that each congregation, when a minister is normally inducted to a charge, presents him or her with a call, signed personally by the members indicating the great need they have felt to have a 'fixed pastor', and they take vows to support the ministry and to pray that their pastor may be guided, inspired and upheld by Christ. Above all they are meant to have a deeply felt concern to hear and to be given insight into the Word of God. John Knox in his history of the Reformation in Scotland[7] speaks of how greatly he himself was inspired in his preaching by the 'hunger of the people' everywhere for the Word. It is this desire that is still meant to be the dominant motive which draws

[7] Cf. Letter from St. Andrews, June 23, 1559; also A. G. Dickens, *The Reformation in England*, p.243.

people towards their pastor. The evidence of such a response to his or her outgoing pastoral concern is obviously a great encouragement to the pastor and will even affect his or her study of the Word, and the preparation and delivery of the sermon. A Scottish clergyman, David Dickson, well known in his day, spoke of how much he had depended, during two periods of ministry, on what he called the 'pastoral intercourse' between himself and his people. One congregation he found more open and encouraging to his pastoral ministry and preaching than the other, and he affirmed that it took him only hours to prepare a sermon for them, whereas it had taken days to prepare a sermon for the other. He lamented moreover that when he became a professor of divinity and no longer had a congregation of his own his preaching fell off in 'sweetness and force'. 'No wonder', he said, 'I've lost my books!' Those of us today who have had experience of various ministries and then have been switched to a less pastoral work, like teaching, will be well able today to understand this testimony. This two-way pastoral tie and the prayer for each other, the ardent desire to seek and find, the listening and looking together, and the hearing and seeing together, are the most important aspects of the interpretation of the Scriptures within the congregation.[8]

We have to remember, however, that the lay membership of the congregation are meant to be not simply passively supportive but also vocal. We began this chapter by affirming the part which the laity must have alongside the pastors in the interpretation of the Bible. We had in mind the ideal expressed in this matter some years ago in a book on theological

---

[8]   J. J. Von Allmen, in *Preaching and Congregation*, p. 52, speaks of how much the ministry of preaching is compromised if it is not part of pastoral work. He gives it as his opinion that the pastor should be wary of exchanging his pulpit even occasionally with a friend or a neighbouring pastor for 'one cannot prepare a sermon away from the parish to which it is to be addressed'. He expresses his pity for the travelling preacher who has no opportunity of addressing the same congregation at least every fortnight.

education: 'We require a community of shared experience and mutual edification and correction to take place'.[9] The restoration of the pastoral cell-group within the Church could be a development of great importance if it helped to bring about such an ideal within Church life.

It should be accepted far more readily than it is in the Church today that God has given us in Holy Scripture a book, the essential message of which can become as clear to the layman as to the pastor. One of the Reformed confessions maintains the doctrine of the 'clarity of Holy Scripture' in words that apply in this context: 'God has so tempered the style and phraseology in the Scripture that those things which contain faith, morals, hope and love may be found placed openly in Scripture, and may be discerned by all according to the calling and measure of faith to be applied to themselves savingly. There are mysteries, but these have been recorded in clear language' (John 7:17-18).[10]

The lay person is of course today always seriously listened to where practical matters like finance and community organisation are concerned and especially today is given the leadership where expert scientific and medical knowledge is required for important ethical decision. Yet it is not always realised that even in order to hear what the spirit is saying to the churches at every level of its life and activity the Church is meant to be as dependent on the shared insight of its whole membership as it is on those who are called to the ordained ministry. Moreover, it is brought out in many translations of Ephesians 4:11-12 that it is the duty of pastors in the Church not to monopolise 'the work of the ministry' to which they are called, but also to 'equip the saints' for that very task. This implies that they must spend time training at least selected members of the congregation in their own interpretative skills.

It should be remembered, moreover, that there have been important and beneficial times in the history of the Church when a large proportion of the ordinary capable lay

---

[9] Cf. *Achievement in Theological Education* - Essays by Niebuhr, Williams and Gustavson, p.96 ᴸ ᵩ

[10] *Leiden Synopsis*. Cf. Heppe, *Reformed Dogmatics*, p.62.

membership did take a decisive part in the outcome of important theological discussion within the Church. R. P. C. Hanson in his study, *Allegory and Event,* has pointed out that the enormous popularity of the writings of Origen in his day proves that the ordinary laymen then fully understood the kind of theological discussion which would be thought the exclusive province of the expert today, and has thus raised the question why what then was such a lay concern should no longer be so. Karl Barth has raised the same question in his recently translated book on Calvin, pointing out that the catechism for children which he issued in Geneva and is today regarded as too difficult for even adults to understand was at that time by no means so, but was exactly on their wavelength. It *was* understood, he affirms. 'The whole history of Geneva for the next centuries proves that. The Genevans quickly learned to listen to Calvin on predestination and Christ's eucharistic presence, and to speak about it themselves, just as the manual workers and barbarians of Byzantium and Alexandria could speak about *homoousios* and *homoiousios.* Such things were for them not just pettifogging issues or matters for doctors of theology, but living questions. If they no longer are that for us, so much the worse for us!'[11] Barth's inclination at this point is severely to blame the generations of laity who allowed this state of affairs to develop for their cupable indifference and blindness to the most important issues of their time. In his *Dogmatics* he insists again that the level of theological understanding among the laity should be as high as it ever is among the ordained ministry in a challenge he issues to the laity themselves. He accuses them today of renouncing 'the freedom which is offered under the word' and of wishing 'to live only by authority in the Church'. 'Those who are silent in deference to Scriptural learning, the congregation which is passive in matters of Biblical exegesis, is', he affirms, 'no longer a true congregation of Jesus Christ'.[12]

Yet the laity is by no means entirely to blame. The deference which the Church has come to pay too much to its trained

[11]   *The Teaching of Calvin, p.256.*
[12]   C.D. 1/11 pp. 414-415.

experts working in isolation has been due too often to an authoritarian and self-confident attitude on their part. Those of us who are pastors today should on our part be continually aware of how much we can receive from the laity through the fellowship they are often willing to give us as they respond to our ministry. According to Paul it is only when each of us steps out of our isolation and seeks fellowship 'with all the saints' that we will begin to be able adequately to appreciate the whole range and depth of the love of God in Christ and become open both to understand and to receive the fullness of what God is seeking to give us (cf. Eph. 3:17-19). The pastor in his or her preparation for the forthcoming service within the congregation can receive beforehand both encouragement and insight through the prayers of the people and the pre-discussion with them of the text. Moreover, we as pastors must hold it possible that some of our lay hearers may have seen what we have witnessed to with greater clarity than we ourselves have experienced. They may indeed have found in the Gospel a meaning we ourselves have not yet seen. And they can help us to enlarge the experience we have already sought to share. It can thus become possible for us to discover fresh aspects of the 'manifold wisdom of God' (Eph. 3:10) within our Church fellowship.

Here again we can refer to the opportunity for mutual sharing and correction that can take place in the growing number of Study and House groups within the Church. When other aspects of Church life are waning, the encouragement these give for the laity to speak and the pastor to listen may be a heartening sign that God is concerned to reform us as he renews us.

The Reading of the Word of God

Under the leadership of Ezra when the people of Israel were going through a period of depression and perplexity, and no prophets seemed to be there to give them encouragement and guidance, they decided to search their Scriptures to see what the ancient law of Moses had to say to them (Neh. 8:1-18). The way in which they heard the Word which uplifted their morale and transformed their situation is instructive. The interpretation took place in the context of the worship which then was customary in their community life. They built a pulpit of wood so that the Scriptures could be heard by everybody as they were read aloud. The translation given in the RSV of the ministry of the Levites suggests that there were two quite distinct stages in what took place: 'So they read from the book, from the law of God with interpretation. They gave the sense so that the people understood the reading' (v. 8). The first part of the description implies that an interpretation was first given simply in the way the text was read. It was to an already significant reading that comments were afterwards added to give further elucidation. It has been pointed out by R. E. Palmer[13] that the vocal reading of an important literary text can enable it to become 'a meaningful oral happening in time', or a 'word event' in which its true nature and integrity can show forth, and there is no doubt that Paul's letters and many of the oracles of the prophets were at least written to be read in this way.

In our evaluation of what takes place in public worship we have to appreciate more than is often done that the sympathetic and intelligent reading of the Scriptures by the ordinary member of the Church who has an aptitude for such a task can by itself become an illuminating and powerful means of their interpretation and is meant by God to be such. I myself, time and again, as I have listened to the reading of a passage in Church have found myself especially arrested by the way in which particular phrases or sentences can force themselves on the attention and link up with each other, often in a way that would not occur through private study or devotional reading.[14]

---

[13] In his very helpful book, *Hermeneutics.*

[14] Cf. P. C. Bori, From Hermeneutics to Ethical Consensus. Atlanta Ga, 1994, where reading is described as an act which generates infinite meanings, which spring from connections between the texts, and between the texts and the reader. (We would add also 'the hearer'). In the life of Robert Leighton there is quoted a minute of the Synod of Dunblane, 9 Oct 1664, in which people are urged to listen to the 'publick reading of Scripture more reverentlie and more religiouslie, with the assurance that they will not fail to find ... divers pasages and sentences falling frequentlie in upon their hearts ... with particular warmth and divine force, below, if not sometimes beyond, what they usually find in private.' *Life of Robert Leighton,* by R. Butler, p.376.

It is important to remind ourselves again that in order to be fully interpreted, texts have to be resounded and listened to, as well as analysed and explained historically and devotionally. Expression is an important part of interpretation. Though it is possible to describe in a lecture or an article, the intentions of the composer of a piece of music, the work has to be performed to be interpreted. I recall my experience as a student listening to Sir Herbert Grierson interpreting poetry. He spent time going over parts of it explaining why it was written, and what he believed the author was trying to say. Then time and again he finished up by reciting the poem or significant parts of it, seeking to communicate how it had come home to himself. Though our own aims, in giving a passage of Scripture such expression, are much more far-reaching than anything in the mind of a literary critic seeking to evoke the emotions behind the original utterance or to unfold the thoughts that lay behind it, there is nevertheless a lesson to be learned from this example from the secular world. There is much to be said for the older homiletic method of preaching, in which a longer portion of Scripture than is often customary today, is chosen as a text. The preacher, without any attempt at 'introduction', begins at the beginning of the passage and follows through it, discussing whatever relevant point arises in the sequence and occasionally resounding the portion of the text under discussion to make sure that one is on the rails and that the people are really hearing what it says. How enriching it can be to our people that through the use of a prescribed liturgy as much as possible of the Bible should be regularly opened up before the minds of the faithful and given such interpretative expression in public worship!

CHAPTER 7

THE INTERPRETATION OF THE TEXT

(ii) The Use of Human Skills and Resources

Criticism

It is commonly accepted that we can be helped to find out the meaning of the Biblical writings by the methods used commonly in all literary criticism. To 'criticise' anything, can of course mean to point out its faults and it has to be admitted that sometimes those who use critical methods on the Bible allow this aim to come to mind, and use their skills for this purpose. The word criticism, however, in a literary context, is more often used positively and denotes an effort to bring out the merits of a work. F. F. Bruce points out that the use of critical methods is 'of great service in the study of the Bible'. The whole subject is often discussed under four headings: Textual Criticism, Literary and Historical Criticism, Redaction Criticism and Form Criticism.

In the brief compass of this book our discussion must focus mainly on the use of literary and historical criticism and we do this under the name commonly adopted for it in our next heading. Briefly, however, in passing we can indicate that textual criticism arises out of the fact that the early manuscripts which have come down to us often differ through errors of the copyists who made them from a more original or perhaps from *the* original source. Sometimes these errors were unintentional, sometimes deliberate, owing to the scribe's not liking what was originally written. Textual criticism seeks to find out by a survey of all the manuscripts before us what the most genuine may have been. Redaction criticism deals with the fact that parts of the books that have come down to us passed on their way through the hands of an editor, and that whole books may have been finally edited as a whole before they achieved their ultimate form. The critic seeks to find out where we can trace the hand of such an editor or where the document might have been allowed to come to us from the original author.

Scholars using the method of form-criticism seek to show us how the form of some of the documents and literary compositions which occur in the Bible can be compared with similar compositions and documents in common circulation and use in the world around at the same time. What we know and can discover of the meaning of these writings and compositions can thus cast light on the Biblical examples. Recently much work has been done by critics trying to probe the possible meaning of the Bible stories by examining various forms in which they are written. Behind this research there is the belief that it was common in that earlier world for the story teller to shape the story according to the kind of lesson he wanted to teach. The accepted use of a particular form in a secular context may therefore cast light on the use of that form in a Biblical context.[1]

The Grammatico-historical Approach to the Text

For many generations the interpretation of the Bible within the Church has been dominated by what has come to be called the 'Grammatico-historical method'. It can be claimed that the vast number of Biblical commentaries, guides and dictionaries which fill our book shops and libraries and find their place on the shelves and desks of our pastors, owe much of their contents to the use of this method. The purpose for which they were written is to explain what the words and sentences of the text mean as they occur and lie in their context.

---

[1] The Pontifical Biblical Commission report on *The Interpretation of the Bible in the Church,* Boston 1993, lists 'New Methods of Biblical Analysis' described as 'Rhetorical Narrative', and 'Semiotic' and also lists 'New Approaches that use the human sciences'.

They also seek to inform us as adequately as possible about the circumstances under which the texts were written and the situation of the people addressed or involved. They seek to explain 'the original intention of the writer' of the document or book. We are given important information about the psychology and sociology of the Semitic world to which he belonged and the pervading religious beliefs in which he might have shared. They can show us how these seem to be akin to, and yet are different from, contemporary alien religions.

We must welcome the work and the results of such scholarship. As we read Israel's history it can help us greatly to have an accurate knowledge of the pagan customs of the surrounding nations, of what was going on in contemporary history, of the geographical background of the incidents we have to study. As we seek to understand the New Testament epistles it is useful to know the exact circumstances in which Paul wrote his letters and of what might have been the uppermost concern in his mind. When I read the book of Isaiah for the first time, seeking to learn it for my entrance Bible exam, I was greatly puzzled, finding I could not make clear sense of much that I read — until someone suggested I should read one of the current commentaries which held and thrilled me so much that I won an unexpected welcome first prize which was posted to me as the result. It has pleased God to speak through articulate human speech which we can equip our minds to study, and we must be prepared to meet him on the ground on which he has chosen to meet us.

One of the chief services done for the Church by the expert in language and history through the skills we are here discussing, is of course the production of a worthy translation of the Biblical text. Other factors, theological and literary, besides accurate scholarship must play their part in deciding the final form of such a translation but it must above all be justified by the method we are here discussing.[2]

---

[2]   No translation can be regarded as final. That there are so many slightly different ones around today can be a help to us if we carefully study the slight differences between those which have the most reliable reputations for their scholarship.

There is no doubt that the influence of commentaries produced by this critical method has for many generation been dominant in the interpretation of Scripture given in the pulpits of our Churches, and volumes of such commentaries continue to be found useful. Yet there has been a growing tendency to raise various question over the limitation of the field of research open to it. The commentators, says Sarna, tend to close their minds to 'that elusive indefinable essence which is beyond the scope of their method'.[3] They fail to recognise in the Bible 'a dimension not accessible to the ordinary means of investigation'. Certainly they can often bring before us in a marvellously impressive way the concrete details of the history, the political and social forces which seemed to dominate what was happening and the motivating issues in the minds of the persons involved. Yet at the same time they too often fail to appreciate the presence within the history of the intrusive power of the Word of God as it time and again dominated the whole flow of events and oriented it towards the coming of Christ and his salvation. 'Neither will any concentration of attention on Isaiah or Paul', says Richard Neibuhr, 'any detailed understandingof their historical situation, enable the observer to see what they saw. One must look *with* them and not *at* them to verify their visions, participate in their history rather than regard it, if one would apprehend what they apprehended'. The Bible, Karl Barth points out, 'represents men as constrained and subjugated by a truth which has laid hold of them: they speak of a revelation they have received and turn their eyes to a revelation that is to come. This is something which modern commentaries do not and cannot explain. Recourse must then be had to the earlier commentaries, especially those of Calvin and Luther'.[4] The critical scholar who

---

[3] N. Sarna, *Understanding Genesis*, p.xxv.

[4] Cf. Barth , *Prayer and Preaching*, p.103; Richard Niebuhr, *The Meaning of Revelation*, p.73. Cf. H. Schlier, *Dogmatic and Biblical Theology*, p.93: 'The historical and philological appraoch is never enough to disclose the sense of a historical text .... one must always be involved in the reality which confronts us in the texts of the New Testament'. Cf. also J. D. Smart, *The Interpretation of Scripture*, p.51.

tends to claim to have the last word to say on a passage of Scripture deserves the rebuke of Augustine: 'At best thou art an eye, thou art not the light and what good is even an open and sound eye, if the light be wanting?' [5]

For critical scholarship to play its fully effective part within the life of the Church, the scholar is meant to be aware of this, and of the call to be more open, than has recently been the case, to listen to what is being said elsewhere in the living fellowship of the Church, perhaps even on matters about which he or she may be an acknowledged expert. The commentaries of Calvin which are markedly different from those we have been discussing here, have obviously been written with great respect for the grammatical and historical sense of the passage. At the same time they took full account of the word that was to be 'heard' and 'seen' within the contemporary Church.

Further considerations should be in our mind when we determine the place which the critical commentary is meant to have in preparation for our ministry. The most zealous advocates of the critical method make it one of their chief rules that the first aim of the interpreter must be that of finding out the intention of the original author when the words of the text were penned. We believe we have good grounds from which to question the wisdom of adhering to such an aim even when the interpretation of any literature is concerned. I have found even in my own attempts to write, that words and sentences are quite often better, and have a richer meaning, on paper than they have had in my mind and as C. H. Dodd said, 'It would not be true of any literature which deserves to be called great, that its meaning is restricted to that which was explicitly in the mind of the author when he wrote.' As time goes by 'ever new richness of unsuspected meaning'[6] can be unfolded as the tradition of the community expands, and this is especially true of those who lived under the impact of the Word of God

[5]   Serm. in N.T. XVII 8 p.155.
[6]   C. H. Dodd, *According to the Scriptures*, pp.131ff. On the point see especially J. T. Wilkinson, *Interpretation and Community*, p.205, on 'The ineradicable difference between what is thought and what is said'!

in Israel's developing religious culture. Thus it happens that we ourselves are able to find a wealth of meaning in an ancient text of the Bible that was not even discernible when it was originally written. What it means as part of the Bible is of much more importance than what it originally meant — and are we not on good ground when we say that God had this future meaning in mind when he inspired the original utterance?[7]

It must be admitted that even where a text could be found to cast valuable light on God's purpose for salvation, enlarge our vision and give us insight into God's purpose for our lives, the comments made in the kind of commentary we are discussing often give us only background information, much of which is only of antiquarian value.[8] It is important therefore that we should be well aware of the limitations that a strict adherence to this method constantly imposes on those who are dedicated to its use. I was once greatly disappointed when we invited a very popular preacher from our city to our chapel service at our Seminary, and sat there hoping to hear a fresh and helpful word for our need. He simply said, 'I would not dream of exegeting a text of Scripture before so many experts', and gave his views on the general Church situation in the area. 'No one', writes Herbert Butterfield, 'would expect a scholar,

---

[7] N. P. Williams, in the *Doctrine of the Fall and Original Sin,* points out that on this subject the New Testament writers 'found in the Old Testament a deeper meaning than ever th Jews had found', and he quotes from one Oxford sermon of H. L. Goudge: 'What the words *originally meant* matters little, what they *mean as part of the Bible* matters a great deal.' J. T. Wilkinson, *Op. Cit.,* p.175, points out how deeply Augustine was concerned that an interpreter of Scripture should try to find out what the author wanted to say (Confessions XII, 18), yet he meditates while he does this: 'What harm is there, light of all truthful minds if he understands what thou dost show to be true, even though the author failed to see it, since he also will have understood a truth, though not this one?'

[8] 'The background', it has been observed, 'has too often been made the foreground'. Thomas Mertoun speaks of the 'stupidity and bad taste of a generation of commentators who have a talent for burying essentials under useless details'. Cf. *Bread in the Wilderness,* p.26.

by reason of his technical accomplishments, to be more skilled than other people in making love or choosing a wife.'[9]

The Theological Approach[10]

This approach to the interpretation of Scripture arises from the belief that there is a rationality and an unchangeable unity in God himself which is reflected in his Word. Everywhere in the Bible the basic understanding of all its .writers and editors about the nature of God, his purpose and ways in his creative and redeeming activity, are the same. It is this theological unity that enables us, as we have already noted, to interpret what one writer has said by our knowledge of what other writers are saying. We can be helped to interpret one part by what another teaches, and also by what the whole Bible teaches. 'An exposition is tustworthy', says Barth, 'to the extent that it not only expounds the text before it but implicitly, at least, all other texts'.[11] This is, of course, especially useful in the interpretation of those places where the meaning is obscure, for we can be helped to interpret them by what other texts in similar contexts teach clearly.

It therefore follows that if our minds can be fully informed and our thinking adequately controlled by a theology that is itself a true reflection of the teaching of the whole of Scripture, we will be greatly helped in our search for the meaning of any part of the Bible. This was a conviction strongly held by John Calvin who began to have a very strong influence on the movement of the Reformation in many parts of Europe, almost a generation after it began in Germany and Switzerland under Luther and Zwingli. In 1536 he published in Basle the first edition of a decisively important work which he kept revising and expanding throughout his life. In the preface to the second edition of this work he affirms that his aim in writing it was to

---

[9]   *Christianity and History,* p.25.
[10]   We are aware that the reader will find little similarity between what is discussed in this section, and what is in the recent book, *Theological Hermeneutics, Development and Significance* by Werner Jeanrond, London 1994.
[11]   Church Dogmatics, II/1, p.485.

help his readers to understand the 'whole of the Christian religion in all its parts' so that those who give themselves to the study of theology should have 'easy access to the reading of the Holy Scriptures' and 'make good progress in the understanding of it'. Calvin regarded the study of theology as giving us a key to the Scriptures. When he wrote his commentary to the Epistle to the Romans he expressed his belief that if we could fully take in the meaning of this Epistle it would greatly help us in the interpretation of any other part of the Bible.

It is important of course that the theology we use in the method here under discussion should never become a dead lifeless orthodoxy learned by rote, or from books on the subject. It must be a theology which we ourselves in our own experience have found to arise out of, and have tested against the widest possible range of Biblical writing. Ideally, of course, the whole of Scripture should be at the back of our mind, influencing our theology and our thinking even as we use our theology.[12] Augustine insists that if we are to be good interpreters the whole of Scripture should be committed to memory, which counts for so much that, 'if the memory is defective no rules can supply the want'.[13] Hunter points out that Calvin could successfully pursue this method because he had such a 'perfect acquaintance with the whole range of Scripture'. 'With an extraordinary tenacious memory, with an intellect of equally remarkable associating power, anything in the nature of a concordance was for him almost unnecessary; he could summon at command any relevant text to illuminate a text or to illustrate a passage'.[14] One of Calvin's ideals for the pastor

[12] Within my own memory one of the chief developments in the study of the Bible has been the appearance of important and massive Biblical studies, not on individual books of the Bible, but on the unity of the New Testament, on the Theology of the Old Testament in general, all leading to a greater awareness within the Church of the unity of the Bible as a whole, and of its witness to salvation history. 'We face the undeniable fact that so very often the best "historical" exegesis is achieved from a theological point of view' — Von Rad, *Essays in Old Testament Hermeneutics,* p.38.

[13] In his work, *On Christian Doctrine.*

[14] A. Mitchell Hunter, *The Teaching of Calvin,* p.19.

was that he should allow his mind to be 'completely moulded' by Holy Scripture.

If our theology is partial and inadequate, what we derive from the Scripture we interpret by its use will of course also be partial and inadequate. We can take warning from the Pharisees. The interpretation given to the Scriptures by John the Baptist led him towards the truth. He recognised Jesus and welcomed him. In the case of the Pharisees their theology had become a tradition so partial, and indeed perverted, that they rejected the Christ to whom their Scriptures bore clear witness. Jesus in accusing them exposed their shortcomings and the root of their blindness: 'For the sake of your tradition you make void the Word of God' (Matt. 15:6). Here in these solemn words we can read not only a warning in case our own theology is partial and one-sided, but also in case our theology, however adequate in form, has become in our use of it a mere lifeless dogma — just a 'tradition'! — and has taken a place in our mind and devotion prior to Scripture itself. While we use our theology to help us to understand the text we must be always more open to what the text says than to what our theology says. Calvin said simply that our theology can be of help in giving guidance about 'what to look for' when we face a text of Scripture. What we find as we look may, however, be something quite different from or even contrary to what we were looking for. We must therefore always be willing to have our theology, as we use it, corrected by what it finds in the text of Scripture and especially kept alive by the texts that tend to question and correct it — a theology continually itself being reformed by the Word of God.[15]

The Enlistment of Imagination and Insight

A book widely circulated in the USA some years ago gave the result of a 'nationwide inquiry among eminent mathematicians'.

---

[15] It is at this point that we have to be aware of the deterioration that took place in the Church's life because it followed the way taken too easily even by Augustine who was so confident in what he had in his Church theology and practice already, apart from Scripture, that he required Scripture 'only for the purpose of instructing others'. (On Christian Doctrine, 1:39).

It reported that 'all of them thought neither in verbal terms, nor in algebraic symbols, but relied on visual imagery of a hazy kind'.[16] It spoke of 'sudden leaps of creative imagination', and 'spontaneous intuitions and hunches of unconscious origins'. God himself is well aware that there are people in the world gifted to respond in such a way to the problems and opportunities with which their minds can be confronted, and we cannot imagine that in giving us his Word in Holy Scripture he would narrowly restrict the kind of response he is seeking from the human mind to be always carefully thought out and pursued, only following steps which can be regarded as scientific and logical. In facing the interpretation of the Bible we have, at some point in the discussion, to take account of what H. J. C. Grierson refers to as the small part played by reason in the life of most men, and the enormous potency of the imagination.[17]

It is obvious that in the narrative portions of the Bible the authors are not primarily concerned to give us always clearly and factually presented accounts which can be classed as 'history' in the scientific understanding of that term. Even their history is presented to us in story after story, some of which can be classed as great literature. We can claim that in order to appreciate it in the fullness of its humanity we can profit from the same kind of skill that literary critics today bring to bear on the works that come under their review in the realm of modern literature. A recent writer on Rudyard Kipling defines the gift which made him esteemed as both a critic and story teller as 'a spontaneous insight into the nature of an event or situation or whatever'. It is the gift of enabling people to see something significant where before they were able humanly speaking to see very little. 'The critic to whom I am most grateful', says T. S. Eliot, 'is the one who can make me look at something I have never looked at before, or looked at with eyes clouded with prejudices, set me face to face, and then leave me with it' [18]

---

[16] *The Ghost in the Machine*, pp.180–181.
[17] *Cross Currents in English Literature*, p.29.
[18] *On Poets and Poetry*, p.117.

Of course there is always danger in actively encouraging the use of imagination in the interpretation of Scripture and we will not hesitate to point this out when we deal with the subject of 'allegory'. Jonathan Edwards in his day was often faced by those who were too ready to 'find some text of Scripture suddenly and extraordinarily brought to their minds', and he quaintly and profoundly laid down the rule, that rightly to interpret Scripture is to understand 'what was in it before it was understood', i.e. 'what used to be contained in the meaning of it and not to make a new meaning'.[19] Yet perhaps Edwards relied too heavily on logic. There is truth in C. S. Lewis' observation that 'symbols are the material speech of the soul, a language older and more universal than words',[20] and there is certainly wisdom in his warning against that 'rationalizing spirit' which gives us only 'victory over the inanimate, while calling us off from the depth of our own nature'. 'Our lives', writes Hatch, 'are hedged about by the unknown' and 'even the human facts of life are linked up with infinity'.[21] It is in place at this point to quote Von Rad's defence of typological interpretation which later we will further study in detail: 'Without this analogical sort of thinking there would be no poetry. The poet goes ceaselessly to and fro; he sees the often insignificant, obvious things and recognises in them ultimate value. In the movements of the elements, the passing of the years and the days, in the most elementary relationship of man with man, in simple mechanical performances — in everything regularity "reveals" itself and hints at an order that dwells deep within things'.[22]

'Let us apply ourselves to the text', says Barth. 'The true exegete will always find in it fresh depths and new mysteries, like a child in a marvellous garden he will be filled with wonder'.[23]

[19] *On the Religious Affections*, p.207.
[20] *Mediaeval Literature*, p.137
[21] Hibbert Lectures, p.84.
[22] *Essays in Old Testament Typology*, p.17.
[23] *Prayer and Preaching*, p.16.

CHAPTER 8

THE APPLICATION OF THE WORD

Finding the Way

God is concerned to speak to us through the Bible not only about the truth in which we are to believe but also about the way we have to take in obedience to his will. As he utters his word he seeks not only to reveal himself to the world, but also to reconcile, to renew and control it. He seeks to involve us in this work. We expect therefore to find through our reading and interpretation of the Bible, directions about the way of life that accords with our faith.

B. Nagy observes that finding the way is a learning process in face of our continually changing life-situations. 'What we learn through the Bible', he says, 'is not only the Gospel of Jesus Christ but the distinctive way of life which he creates among men, and we must continually re-learn its meaning in concrete situations.' When he wrote these words for publication in a collection of articles over forty years ago, the use of the nuclear bomb had begun to raise ethical questions in our minds and was beginning to force us to revise out thinking on a matter about which it had seemed to be settled. Many of us, up till then had felt it possible for our country to become engaged with honour in a war, provided the cause was just and our forces avoided all inhuman atrocity. The manufacture and unleashing of the nuclear bombs on Hiroshima and Nagasaki, however, made us begin to question what had become in our minds an ethical certainty. The Church today is faced with several no less perplexing problems by the recent advances in genetic engineering. Moreover, as individuals, in a way not thought possible in previous generations, our minds are being challenged by a flood of radical new thinking in the sphere of sexual relations to examine whether our settled convictions on such matters have been right or wrong. What are we to think? What way are we to take? Even though we may believe that in the realm of truth there may be things final and absolute, are there such in the realm of morality?

The author of the Epistle to the Hebrews helps us towards a valid understanding of why we may be experiencing such sudden and devastating change in our common religious and social life today. He points out that at times when men and women have begun to feel too securely established in idolatrous and false ideas, God shakes things up and allows whatever is not solidly founded on his word to collapse in order to prove their untrustworthiness. He shakes things up, the sacred writer says, 'so that what cannot be shaken may remain' (Heb. 12:26–28). In all such times of upheaval and change under God's hand, the solid things of eternal value prove their stability and worth!. They are there — 'the same yesterday, today and for ever'. God, even at a time like this, has not left us to grope our way tentatively from one .nervous decision to another. As we search the Scriptures he will enable us to find and teach our day and generation that 'distinctive way of life which Jesus Christ creates among men' and which marks us out as Christians

This distinctive way of life has to be continually learned and 'relearned'. It is not a way that can be codified in a final set of rules, abstracted from the whole Bible in a selection of Biblical texts, or defined principles.[1] We must always allow the settled ideas about morality and even religion which we have lived by to be put to the test as they become challenged in face of the changes which God is allowing to come about around us. We have to turn always afresh to Scripture We have to ask that it may be given, to seek that we may find and to knock and wait that it may be opened to us! We have to find out whether our

---

[1]   The article by James Muilenburg in *Biblical Authority Today* is valuable in this connection. He points out that what is often demanded of the reader of the Bible is an understanding of the 'concrete historical context' of incident after incident. 'The Bible is a sacred history, and a distilling of permanent laws and principles from it is not in keeping with its fundamental meaning', p.214.

certainties can really come to us again as fresh certainties which arise out of a deeper and clearer understanding of the Scriptures than we had before.

Even the Old Testament prophets and those who believed they had the 'law' of God to live by, could feel at times that they were walking 'in darkness with no light' (Isa. 50:10) except a little 'lamp at their feet' to ensure they didn't trip up (Ps. 119:105) Paul was no doubt referring to the same difficulty in finding ethical solutions to the problems before us where he warned us each to work out our own salvation in fear and trembling (Phil. 2:12) and to learn to walk by faith and not by sight (2 Cor. 5:7–8). To walk by faith that has been forced to research the Scriptures to find the way does not mean that we do not walk by certainty. The word which we continue to hear will give us fresh certainty.

The Constraint of the Truth

It has to be emphasised first of all that we begin to know the way as we begin to grasp the truth. Our ethics arise out of our doctrine. 'The love of Christ controls us' (2 Cor. 5: 14 — AV has 'constrains'), says Paul, 'because we are convinced that one has died for all, therefore all died'. It was his conviction about the meaning of the atonement that constrained and enabled him to live from then on, not for himself but for others.

In the Epistle to the Romans it is only after many chapters discussing doctrine that he begins to give advice about living the Christian life, and the advice he gives is based entirely on what he has said in the doctrinal section. The same order of discussion is largely taken in his other epistles. When he speaks of the commands of God he brings out that to obey them is simply a 'reasonable' service arising out of the Gospel (Rom. 12:1) and he appeals to his readers to 'discern' what is the will of God by holding before their minds all the great things he has done for them (Rom. 12:2). The same order of discussion is taken and the same motive of behaviour can be seen to be set before his readers in the other epistles. We have to 'live in a manner worthy of the Gospel of Christ' (Phil. 1:27) The nature of the relationship between Christ and his Church, indissoluble, irreversible and eternally faithful, is to be the model we have to hold before us in our thoughts and decisions about marriage (Eph. 5:25 ff) and our sexual behaviour is to be decided by the fact that we are the 'temple of the Holy Ghost' (1 Cor. 6:19). Because of our union with Christ, our bodies which are his members which must not be devoted to any kind of fornication or adultery (1 Cor. 6:15). The grace of God has appeared, not only to bring salvation but to train us in how we must live (Cf. Titus 2:11). We are to imitate God, forgiving one another as he has forgiven us (Eph. 4:32)

In the Old Testament too we find the kind of advice given to us to copy God. Since they themselves were loved, cared for and delivered when they were strangers in the land of Egypt, so they too must likewise love the stranger (Deut. 10:19 — NEB has 'alien'). While the New Testament stresses that our attitude towards the perhaps unknown people around us has to be determined by the fact that each is 'one for whom Christ died' (Cf. Rom. 14:15), it is in the Old Testament that we are introduced to the more universally used and no less powerful ethical motive that God created humankind in his own image (Gen. 1:27). The 'essential law for man is that he shall reflect the image of God, and become like him in character', says H. H. Rowley.[2] The abhorrence expressed by the prophet like Amos of the savage brutality of the genocide perpetrated by foreign nations in their unnatural crimes arises because he feels that the passionate disgust that has arisen within him against such atrocities is not a naturally personal feeling but has been born within him through his communion with God himself and his knowledge of what God is like (Amos 1–2).

Law and Grace in the Ten Commandments

Is it not often our case that when we are acutely conscious of the pressure God is exerting on us in face of a moral issue, we find that pressure coming to us not as the result of a process of doctrinal thinking, but through some Biblical Word which seems to demand of us to take the path we are being shown

---

[2]   Quoted by D. A. Haldane in article on Old Testament Ethics in I.S.B.E.

without argument? In the stories both of the Old and New Testament, we are often shown people who are challenged and tested by God simply to obey commands without being able sometimes to understand the reason why the order was given. It can be argued indeed that if we must always be given good reasons for the behaviour asked of us we are failing to walk by faith. Therefore God ensures that the ethical constraint of the Bible reaches us at times in other ways than through the obedient and grateful reasoning of our minds. God can impress his will directly upon our wills. Obedience is demanded without explanation. His Word can come to us in the form of direct command, prohibition and warning as it came to Adam and Eve in the garden.

The central ethical code which dominates the whole Bible, takes its first grip of our minds in such a form. I remember when I was in Primary School hearing the Ten Commandments read aloud with great solemnity and I had to learn them by heart. I took them personally for they were addressed to each hearer, and undoubtedly the place they took in my mind greatly affected my behaviour. Within our family life too, any breach of them was felt to be much more serious than other more normal forms of misbehaviour. One of my early memories of school life was a rare and special occasion when the Rector of the school was called in to our primary class to rebuke a boy whose misbehaviour had taken the unusual, and in my eyes dreadful, form of directly breaking one of the Ten Commandments. I am quite certain that the effect of the pressure they had on my life and the course it took was immensely stabilising and healthy. I am sure that Luther and Calvin were wise in giving them an important place in the catechetical teaching of the faith to children.

It was many years, however, before I discovered the basically evangelical nature of their ethical constraint. During the early years of my ministry in my first two or three parishes, I felt, as many of my fellow pastors did, that it was our duty to preach through them one by one. An encouragement to do so came from the availability in many second-hand book shops of volumes of ready-made sermons on the subject published by illustrious preachers of the past. In my own expositions I followed the line that they had all taken. I regarded the

Commandments as a comprehensive set of rules defining for all mankind how God had designed life on earth to be lived. They were laws natural to all nations and therefore to be observed with special reverence by his chosen people. I stressed in my sermons that the tone and quality of our social and moral life would greatly degenerate if we neglected to observe them and uphold them in our own civil laws and social behaviour. I remembered that one of my revered teachers at college had affirmed that they gave us an outline of the 'moral constitution of the universe'.

As I came to have a better appreciation of the importance of the witness of the whole Bible to Christ and salvation, I began to ask whether such an interpretation of the commandments was adequate. I was arrested especially by Paul's resolution about his preaching before he went to Corinth: 'I decided to know nothing among you except Jesus Christ, and him crucified'. Was I really justified in spending ten Sundays of a year preaching natural law rather than Jesus Christ? I began to see that the decalogue was the central part of the unique covenant of grace which God entered with his own people as he redeemed them from Egypt. They were not meant to be regarded as setting out the demand of a universal and absolute law for all nations, but as a revelation of the new and liberating kind of life which they were now to enjoy and witness to as his own people. Each command describes an aspect of the freedom now to be enjoyed in the fullness of life which was now opened before God's redeemed people. What was negative about them was indeed a promise that they would continually be given help to overcome all the destructive impulses and forces in their own hearts and would thus no longer *need* to behave as other nations tended to behave. Moreover, the whole wide range of conduct covered by them was a sign that the gracious love and care of God covered every important aspect of life they had to live together.[3]

In discovering the evangelical meaning of the Ten Words, I was, I believe, discovering the original intention of God in giving them to Israel. It was when Jesus Christ came that he

---

[3]   I worked this out in detail in the book I published on *The Ten Commandments — a Study in Ethical Freedom,* in 1964.

revealed in all its fullness the gracious meaning of the commandments as they were originally given. Certainly God has designed them so that they can be at first read and understood as ten 'laws of life', and so understood they can have a helpful and restraining effect for the individuals and social circles which take them seriously. But they are Gospel, and were originally given as Gospel 'in the form and fashion of the law'.[4] We can indeed find some truth in the doctrine that they were the expression of the law natural to all nations. It was Calvin who taught me the important truth that what Christ came to reveal and establish through his life-work and example could be properly understood as the restoration of the humanity we had lost.[5]

Jesus, the Cross and his Teaching

The whole Bible comes to its climax in the account we have in the Gospels of the birth, life, teaching, death and final triumph of Jesus. The Old Testament is a preparation for these happenings, and the Epistles unfold their meaning. It is when we read these Gospel accounts that we are most aware of what Barth refers to as 'the new dimension and radical depths' of the 'divine requirements' which mark the New Testament out in its superiority to the Old.[6]

We must never underestimate how strongly the reader and hearer of the Biblical message can be influenced by both the personal example of Jesus, and by his call to us: 'Follow me'. The word can have two distinct meanings. It was a custom of the time to use it to refer to how the disciple of a revered Rabbi would devotedly follow his way of life and accept and study his teaching. Used by Jesus as he calls his disciples it implies an ardent and intimate personal devotion, a desire to imitate him in all things because he himself *is* the way, and since there is no other who can possibly offer any alternative, a desire always to abide in his friendship, to treasure every word of his teaching

---

4   Cf. Karl Barth, *Church Dogmatics*, II/2 p.511, and *Biblical Authority for Today*, pp.52–53, 95, 237–238, 287.

5   Cf. My *Calvin Geneva and the Reformation, pp. 117–118.*

6   Cf. Karl Barth, *Op. Cit.* II/2 p.697.

with absolute trust. The word 'follow' can also derive its meaning from the promise of Jesus that, alive and exalted in every age to come, he will choose out the path of life that each of his disciples is destined to follow, providentially set them on their way to fulfil it, and go before each one, giving directions and assurance through the hearing of his voice.

We are urged by the Gospel account to keep both meanings of 'follow' in our minds. In both cases we find ourselves under intense ethical constraint. Certainly in what arises from his calling as the Messiah of Israel, and his nature as the Son of God, we are not meant to attempt to imitate him. Yet we are meant to allow ourselves to be drawn to him as a human person and to want ardently to become like him.

As we listen for his voice today we will inevitably hear him at times clearly saying: 'If any want to become my followers let them deny themselves and take up their cross and follow me' (Matt 16:24). We will know then that in the circumstances ahead of us, if we are to take his way, some severe self-denial is urgently being demanded of us, and some kind of cross to be borne is clearly being allocated to us as our lot in suffering. It is not surprising that Calvin when he came to outline in his *Institutes* the ethical implications of the Gospel for personal Christian conduct, he described it under headings derived from his understanding of this text.

We have already in this chapter spoken of how powerfully our grasp of the doctrine of the atonement can constrain us to a life of gratitude to God In order to allow the death of Christ as it is presented to us in the New Testament however, to have its full effect on our lives we have to dwell also on the story of how it happened, to contemplate all the details that are brought before us in the four Gospels of what he suffered as he went through it in his tender sensitive humanity, and open our minds to how deeply God himself was involved in such suffering.[7] As it presents us with both the doctrine and

---

[7]   James Denney, lecturing to his class on the Atonement, said that he envied the Roman priest who could lift up a crucifix before his congregation, and say, 'God loved men and women like that'.

the story of his death, however, the New Testament does not allow us to forget that it was for the joy that was set before him that he endured the Cross, despising the shame, and the confidence of that joy was with him as he endured everything. We ourselves are given an ample foretaste of his resurrection power as we allow ourselves to be involved in the fellowship of his sufferings. It is taken for granted in the New Testament that the Christian in following Jesus will live at times with 'joy unspeakable and full of glory' (1 Pet. 1:8), and is always more than a conqueror in all the adversity that earthly sufferings can bring.

In our search for 'the distinctive way of life which comes to create among us' we must obviously not only allow ourselves to come under his personal influence as he draws us into the fellowship of his death and inspires us with the power of his resurrection. We must also open our minds as fully as we can to his teaching. We cannot do this adequately without giving the priority he himself obviously gave to the Sermon on the Mount. How the sermon affects us will, of course, depend on how we interpret it and some of the commonly accepted ways of interpretation allow us to evade the full impact it was designed by Jesus to have upon us. When I was a youngster and heard it read I tended to think of it as the description of an ideal to be taken seriously only if you really wished to be an exceptionally heroic or indeed a 'perfect' Christian.[8] It was allowable if we felt our vocation was to remain ordinary Christians and to exempt ourselves from the striving and the tension which some of its teaching demanded. When I entered the ministry, and began to preach, however, I was more inclined to accept another of the traditional views, that Jesus, here and there, in the sermon was deliberately seeking to make his demands impossible to fulfil in order to show us how far removed we were from being able to enter the kingdom of God by our own efforts. Indeed they were designed to convict us of our sinfulness and thus incline us to accept or seek the mercy of God.

[8] This was the most commonly held view of it in the middle ages, and a justification for entering monastic orders.

I gradually began to see, however, that these ways of interpreting the sermon tended to rob it of the force it was originally meant to have. Jesus, when he spoke it was not merely painting an ideal picture, and he had no negative purpose in mind. He had no other motive than to demand that all his hearers listen seriously to every part of it and respond with all their heart and mind and strength.[9] It was the occasion of the sermon itself that made me see it this way. It was preached, says Matthew, at the same time and in the setting in which Jesus is described as 'proclaiming the good news of the kingdom and curing every disease and every sickness among the people' (Matt. 4: 23–25). The miracles were themselves good news indeed! — things made possible because the powers of the Kingdom of God were now able to be at work within this world in a new and powerful way through Jesus! The Sermon is also good news indeed! It describes a new way of life now made possible for everyone around Jesus because the evil forces that have dominated so much of this world's life can now be cast down from their place of power by his word! (Luke 11:20–22). The sermon details this new way of life now opened up for everyone who will now hear and allow the demands and promises which Jesus utters to come to full effect in mind, heart and behaviour. People can now become wholly transformed in instinct and character.!

Moreover, at the end of the sermon Jesus makes it clear that all generations to whom the sermon is handed down will be able not simply to *read* these sayings and study them but will be able to *hear* them as spoken by himself. It will happen continually as the sermon is recalled he will be there to re-echo its words with his own voice (Matt. 7:24–27) and the hearing of what these words demand can bring with it the power to effect what is commanded.

The sermon therefore describes the life of a kingdom that has already broken into the world with transforming power. Its demands are the ethics of those who are willing to allow themselves to become caught up more and more fully within the movement of salvation history till Christ comes again. Of

9   Cf the discussion of the sermon in K. Barth, *Church Dogmatics*, II/2 688–692.

course we have to bring to its interpretation all the prayer, scholarly resources and wisdom required in facing all the other parts of the Bible, and such edges in its demands as may be due to deliberate exaggeration, or figure of speech, may be rubbed off in this process. But the immense difficulties of facing up to it will remain to take us out of our depth and tax us beyond our capacity. There is truth in the suggestion that Jesus meant it to be taken as a description of himself. As he showed himself once walking triumphantly on the waves around him to the disciples in the boat, here in another picture of himself he brings out boldly all the outstanding and incomparable features of his own life among men. Of course it is impossible and sometimes foolish for us to imitate him in every aspect of his way of life. Yet when Peter in the boat found his example challenging and told Jesus that he wanted to take the risk, Jesus encouraged him and said, 'Come!'. T. W. Manson, urging us to take the ethical demands of Jesus more seriously reminds us that 'he is there to show the way to all who are ready to follow him'. 'What is more', he continues, 'the strength to follow him is also there. The living Christ has two hands, one to point the way, and the other to stretch out to help us onward'.[10]

The Pervasive Background Influence of Biblical Wisdom and Story

While we are dwelling on the direct ethical thrust of the Word, we must not forget that the influence of the Bible can be powerfully at work at a subconscious level, pervasively shaping the basic desires that lead us to choose the way we take through life. This can happen wherever the family, social and cultural life of a community is open to its influence.

Von Rad, writing a generation ago, makes an illuminating observation about the usual climate which he believed to prevail in the Western world of his day and to influence the ethical decision of men and women even more than categorical imperatives contained in the Ten Commandments or the Sermon on the Mount. 'Every individual always possesses a

[10] T. W. Manson, *Ethics*, p.48.

family, a tribe or a town. The community life has its ethical atmosphere; it compels the individual to live up to specific expectations which people have of him. It provides him with long established examples and values'.[11] John Puddefoot, writing more recently, suggests that within the ideal Christian community it can happen that the children of Christian parents naturally indwell the parental atmosphere and consciously integrate together their unconscious perception of their parents' attitudes and norms and thus acquire, through conversation, precept and story passed on, a non-formal world of thought.[12]

Though I was seldom at Church when I was young, (and I can remember only once being taken to a Sunday School), I am certain that the influence of the Bible came powerfully through in the family and social atmosphere in which I then lived, reached me and affected my thinking even through many of the classroom lessons which I received and the discipline that was exercised during my school life. The advice I received, sometimes casual, sometimes in serious rebuke was quite often indeed reinforced by Biblical texts. I can remember our English teacher warning us not to overrate our abilities, telling us about the battle between Ahab and Benhadad and warning us: 'Let not him that girds on his armour boast himself as he that puts it off' (1 Kings 20:11). Often there was no attempt to preach and I am certain that those who gave us good advice in our life-situation did not know that it came from the Bible. Its influence, however, was there pervading serious conversation. Though my parents did not tell me Bible stories there was current in my home life, many Biblical proverbs and many sensible rules of life which one could call a Christian or Biblical family tradition. Under this influence an almost unconscious shaping of the mind and attitude took place. F. D. Leavis, writing in the 1930's, referred to all this as having been the growth of ages of individual experience of the strongest and most intelligent minds of the community tested by generations of use and pooled to form a stock of social wisdom.

---

[11] In *Old Testament Wisdom,* p.75.
[12] In *Science and the Christian Life,* Ed. T. F. Torrance, pp. 49,46.

Of course the influence which we have described the Bible as having exerted so pervasively on the history of our culture has been as much the creation of the lore of its stories as of its proverbial wisdom. Later in this book we will discuss more fully the story aspect of the Biblical message. At present it is worth while noting that merely by being circulated as stories they can have a powerful influence on our thinking and behaviour. 'The Novelist', said Trollope, 'creeps closer than the schoolmaster. In writing novels, we novelists preach from our pulpit.' R. W. Moberly admirably brings out the point that a story can communicate through assumption and suggestion. He takes the Joseph story and points out how several of the basic features of the message it conveys are not explicitly mentioned — such as God's right and power to send famine, to determine the future, to allow his faithful servants to suffer. The reader who imaginatively enters the story, he affirms, will thereby absorb the same assumptions himself. Such a means of communication, he finally concludes, can be a valuable counterpart to explicit declaration.[13]

I have already referred to the powerful influence of the continual hearing of these stories read to me without comment throughout childhood and adolescence. They kept awake in me the feeling that to live life well was important and that conscience had to be listened to. Like the sayings of Jesus to which I have just referred, they appeared to be full of important warnings about the bondage of simply drifting with the crowd into what the Bible refers to as the 'unclean works of darkness', and about the bitter consequences that can come to ourselves and those dear to us when we break God's law, and they brought assurance that goodness and faithfulness were worth while.

But in the long run, as I gradually absorbed them, they undoubtedly shaped my mind in a way of which I was not conscious, and gave the decisive slant to my thinking and attitude that inclined me towards receiving the Christian faith when it was presented to me in its full significance.

[13] In a magazine article which I cannot now trace.

CHAPTER 9

OPENNESS AND SURRENDER

We earlier reminded ourselves of our need for the Holy Spirit to preside over the whole process of interpretation — especially of our need for him to 'unlock the truth' and reveal the meaning of the texts before us.It is in place here to face a further aspect of work we can expect from his presence.

'No one', warns Luther, 'is able to speak worthily or to hear any part of Scripture if his disposition of mind is not in conformity therewith, so that he feels inside, and cries, "Yes, indeed, that is so!"'[1] Our aim in this present chapter is to sum-up as briefly as possible the 'disposition of mind' which is created in us by the Spirit as he seeks to teach us — openness and surrender.

Receptivity

We have to be open to hear what God is saying to us.I find one aspect of the well-known contrast between Mary and Martha helpful here as an illustration.When Jesus arrived at their house he obviously had something to say and he wanted them to listen.Mary alone understood what was on his mind, dropped her work, sat down, and opened her mind and heart, with adoring receptivity and he spoke to her intimately.In contrast he chided Martha gently for being so 'worried and distracted over many things' that she had missed the 'better part'.Martha in the way she chose, reflects what is too often our own proneness.When we are seeking to interpret Scripture we are

---

[1] W. A. III549.Quoted by A. Skevington Wood in *Luther's Principles of Biblical Interpretation*, p.45.

inclined to immerse ourselves so completely in the exercise of our skills and learning that we fail to be able to discern that he wants to break through all our busyness. What he wants to say doesn't at this time and situation fit into the questions and issues raised in our minds by our skills and method of interpretation. We fail to remember that hearing the Word of God can be a gift as well as a task. Calvin suggests that when Moses approached the burning bush, the command to put off his shoes and approach with reverence, was a reminder that God required of him chiefly the willingness to listen.

We have to become more aware than we sometimes are, of the different ways in which we can fail to be spontaneously and wholly receptive. We have to be aware of how easily we can obscure the message of the Bible by our following of current fashions in the interpretation of secular literature or by our anxiety about the concerns of up-to-date pressure groups around us.[2] We have to be aware of how prone we are to have confidence in ourselves and to approach the text with an inner attitude of superiority towards it. Cullmann reminds us that at times we have to allow the Bible to silence the very questions we bring to it and allow ourselves to face quite other issues than those that are uppermost in our minds.[3] Moreover we have to beware of being led astray even by any favourite method of interpretation. 'No hermeneutic principle', says H. H. Wolf, 'can force the text to testify to God today.' He goes on to insist that, 'No method can replace the Spirit' and that 'our methodology is listening and his activity is speaking'.[4] It is Karl Barth who more forcibly than any other modern theologian reminds us that if we are ready to be open to the contrast

---

[2]   Cf. e.g. the description of the 'New and Fruitful Approaches to Biblical Interpretation' which are to lead Old Testament scholarship into the twenty-first century, listed in the article by C. G. Bartholomew on *Reading the Old Testament in Post-Modern Times*, Tyndale Bulletin, 1998.

[3]   *Salvation in History*, p.70. '*Complete subjection to the text* means ... I must be prepared to hear in faith, an address, running completely contrary to the questions I raise, and in which I do not at first feel myself addressed'.

[4]   *Interpretation*, XV 4p.442.

between the Biblical ideas and our own, all our own certainties, images and ideas must go, and that we ourselves will be overtaken by a peculiar fear and reserve.[5]What is expected of us is defined by Paul: we have to 'take captive every thought to make it obedient to Christ' (2 Cor. 10:5).

The Surrender of 'Every Thought'

Both Luther and Calvin in their discussion of interpretation make us acutely aware of our need for the Holy Spirit not only to reveal the truth but to reconcile us to it as it comes home to us.What hinders us most in our attempts to understand the Word, asserts Calvin, is that we presumptuously bring to it our 'natural shrewdness'.The text, however, can be 'read with advantage' only when we put aside our carnal understanding and subject ourselves to the teaching.[6]

Both Reformers are continually reminding us of our need to be aware of the opposition which continually arises from our own earthly wisdom. Here is an important aspect of our need to deny ourselves.Calvin in a memorable passage in the *Institutes*[7]describes how he faced this conflict as he sought understanding of the text.'We do not with perverted ardor and without discrimination rashly seize upon what first springs to our minds.Rather, after diligently meditating upon it, we embrace the meaning which the Spirit of God offers.Relying upon it, we look down from a height at whatever of earthly wisdom is set against it.Indeed, we hold our minds captive, that they dare not raise even one little word of protest; and humble them that they dare not rebel against it.'

Luther, perhaps a little less severe on our own natural perversity, believed that the devil himself is always at hand to inspire us to find our own beloved falsehoods in what the Scripture says: 'Woe betide all our teachers and authors who go their own merry way and spew forth what is uppermost in their minds, and do not first turn a thought over ten times to be sure it is right in the sight of God.These think that the devil

5   *Church Dogmatics*, I/II p.470.
6   Comm. on 2 Peter 1:20
7   *Inst.* 4:17:25

is away for a while in Babylon, or asleep at their side like a dog on a cushion.They do not consider that he is round about them with all his venomous flaming darts with which he puts into them such superlatively beautiful thoughts adorned with Scripture that they are unaware of what is happening'.[8]

Luther indeed believed that it was a crucial test of the relevance of his preaching that it was such as would continually and consciously confront the opposition and indeed stir it up.The point of relevance in any passage of Scripture was where the thrust of the text conflicted with what people would want to hear.Gustav Wingren points out that for Luther it was the nature of the office of teaching 'that it had its place in the battle between God and the devil, that it *must* have its place there — must continually with conscious intent take its place there'.[9] Indeed if it did not arouse this conflict the preacher had lost touch with the Word.

Whether or not our theology allows us to speak of the devil we have to learn again today that 'the truth of the Bible is known only in conflict'.We have to be aware of our continual tendency to read into the text an alien meaning which our background of thought and culture dictates to us.

The Surrender of the Will

We have given priority in this chapter to the surrender of the mind.We have done so simply to achieve clarity of discussion.There can be no separation of mind from will.In the story of the fall it is the thought of the mind that seems to lead the will into disobedience (Gen. 3:4).When Jesus was being led on to his crucifixion he lamented that our blindness in rejecting him was because we 'were not willing' to have him (Matt. 23:27) and he called on us to be aware that the difficulty

---

8 Luther's Works, E. T. Vol. 37: pp. 17–18
9 *The Living Word, p.95.* This point was well brought out by a prominent Canadian theologian in the 1950's,J. S. Glen: 'Conflict is implicit in the fact that an ideology, like an idolatry, is always in some respect competitive in relation to Biblical truth', *The Recovery of Teaching.*p.72.

we face in interpreting Holy Scripture can lie basically in our unwillingness to do God's will (John 7:17).Athanasius at the end of his *De Incarnatione* reminds Macarius to whom he dedicated the work, that 'for the searching and right understanding of the Scriptures there is need of a good life and a pure soul and for Christian virtue to guide the mind and grasp so far as human nature can, the truth concerning God the Word'.'A person', he concludes, 'wishing to see a city or country goes to the place in order to do so'.[10] Augustine in a confession in one of his sermons is blunt and instructive on this point: 'I am speaking to you who was once deceived, when as in my early boyhood I chose to bring to the divine Scriptures a subtlety of criticising before the godly temper of one who was seeking the truth: by my irregular life I shut the gate of my mind against myself: when I should have knocked for it to be opened,I went on to make it more closely shut, for I dared to search in pride for that which none but the humble can discover.' [11]

---

[10]   *De Incarnatione*, § 57. G. Brendan in a study of *St. John of the Cross*, p.118, recalls the story of a romantic character when riding on the sea-shore with a falcon on his wrist, heard a mariner in a ship singing a magic song that made the winds drop, the sea become calm, the fish rise to the surface and the birds perch on the mast.But when he begged the mariner to teach him that song the man refused: 'I will only tell that song to him who sails with me'.

[11]   *Sermons in New Testament*, E.T. Vol 1: 6p.7.

CHAPTER 10

CENTRAL ISSUES IN INTERPRETATION

Typology

We have already spoken of how time and again the prophets and leaders of Israel felt themselves caught up in a unique and powerfully impelling forward movement towards a great future destiny. When they described their visions of how God was going to work out the future salvation of Israel, the pictures they give us include those of a new exodus through the wilderness (Isa. 43: 18–19) and a new entry into a promised land (Jer. 16:14f), a new and faultless David as king (Amos 9:11, Jer. 23:5), a new and perfect City of God (Isa. 1:21–27, Ezek.40), a new temple with perfect worship (Isa 2:2–4, Ezek 40–46).[1]

Here and there in the Old Testament God so controls and moulds the history of his people that certain features which have prominently marked the past course of events become prophetic of the course he wills it to take as it moves towards the future fulfilment of the promises he made to Abraham and Moses when he called and redeemed them. The great works of God in their past will foreshadow even greater works that God is gong to do for them in their future. They look forward, as G. W. Lampe puts it, 'to a repetition and recapitulation of the rhythm of divine action evident in the history of the past'.[2]

From the time Jesus began his ministry it is obvious that he had in mind for himself such leadership in Israel as would

---

[1]   Cf. D. W. B. Robinson, *The Hope of Christ's Coming*, p.11
[2]   *Typology*, p.26

bring about the fulfilment of all such Old Testament prophecies. His first step in this direction was to choose twelve disciples as a sign that he had an Israel always around him. He encouraged his disciples to think of himself as the true Messianic King, the 'Son of David'. He gave signs that he wanted to be regarded as the new Moses, offering his people the new and perfect law of blessedness on the mountainside and feeding them with the true bread of life, as he led them through the surrounding wilderness towards the promised land.[3]

It was always in his mind from the beginning of his ministry that he was to fulfil the role of 'the servant of the Lord', spoken of so much in the book of Isaiah who would live a life in which he always tended to identify himself with the poor, the sick and the suffering around him, finally choosing to die, bearing and taking away the sin of the world. He spoke of himself frequently as 'going as it was written of him' and finally affirmed that he would come again as the 'Son of Man', 'coming with the clouds of heaven'.

The New Testament writers, looking back over his completed life and work all recognised that God had moulded and used history in this way to 'illumine his purpose' (Ellis) and that thus 'the dumb facts of history had become prophetic' (Von Rad). They recognised that God by his sheer and marvellous grace had forgiven the long-drawn-out centuries of tragic suffering and bitter disappointment caused by the wilful disobedience of his chosen people, and had made possible the replacement of the old covenant by the new, and of the old history of failure by a new one of glorious promise.

---

[3]   It was a commonly held conviction that just before the Messiah came, Elijah would reappear on the earth, and John the Baptist claimed by his manner of life and witness and stress to be such. W. Vischer suggests the possibility that Jesus among his miracles actually did some in a way that made himself look like a second Elisha — the humble miracle worker who followed the great prophet. Jesus thus encouraged John to overcome his doubt by bringing such signs to his notice (Cf. Matt. 11:2–6). This would be an indication of how firmly both regarded salvation history as embedded with such typology. Cf. my *Readings in II Kings*, pp. 60–61.

When the Apostles had been called by Jesus there had begun the election of a New Israel. What had come to them together through Christ in experience and achievement was to them the beginning of the fulfilment of all the great promises of the Old Testament, and they looked forward towards his second coming for the final revelation of the glory of every one of them.

The New Testament thus looks back on the whole history of the old as a prophecy of things to come. Here and there in the Epistles the incidents, things and persons which are regarded as foreshadowing what is future are called 'types' and the forthcoming events and the things or persons they refer to are called 'anti-types'. Francis Foulkes gives an excellent definition of typology. 'A type is an event, a series of circumstances, or an aspect of the life of the individual or of the nation, which finds a parallel and a deeper realisation in the incarnate life of our Lord, in his provision for the needs of men or in his judgments and future reign'.[4] Ellis points out that as well as those types we have already mentioned, Adam (Rom. 5:4), Jonah (Matt. 12:46), and the Paschal Lamb (1 Cor: 5:7) are types of Christ. The Flood, like the Exodus, is regarded as a typical Christian experience (1 Pet. 3:18ff).[5]

We have to recognise a remarkable work of God's hand in forming Israel's history so that it will contain and show such types and anti-types. Calvin, as T. H. L. Parker points out, insists that the primary purpose God had in mind when he created David king was to create within Israel's history such an image of the coming Redeemer. Of course Israel needed such a king as David was to deliver them from the Philistines. Yet he was set there on the throne to make Israel prosper primarily so that its history might contain this important type![6]

That this extraordinary series of promises should be developed in the minds of one particular people about their future destiny, should centre on such a future King Messiah

---

4   *The Acts of God*, p.39.
5   Cf. E. Earl Ellis, *St. Paul's Use of the Old Testament*, p.126.
6   *Calvin's Use of the Old Testament*, pp. 75–76, Cf. *Calvin's Commentary on Psalm 2*.

and should, in spite of persistent difficulties that are always present in working with human nature, become so patiently worked out and embedded in their history, in the life, death and resurrection of Jesus! — all this is I believe a remarkably convincing proof that God himself must have been indeed consistently, closely and powerfully at work here from generation to generation. H. H. Rowley called the typology in the Bible 'a correspondence that is significant and impressive, and one that is unique in history'.[7]

It is unfortunate that the uniqueness of this quite outstanding and marvellous correspondence between the two Testaments, which it was, after all, the life-work of Jesus to confirm and establish, has not always been appreciated. It has, rather, encouraged even highly regarded expositors of the Bible to search in the Old Testament for 'types' which could not possibly have been prominent in Jesus' mind as he was planning his work on earth. We question, for instance, Andrew Bonar's use of typology in his commentary on Leviticus where he claims that each of the sacrifices described in the book was intended by God in its details to be a resemblance to some spiritual truth in the New Testament.[8] What results too often when typology is treated in this way as a method of interpretation is that the skills normally used to find the meaning of a text are neglected and the expositor tends to play games with words and things to force artificial meanings upon texts and incidents. There is a tendency indeed, as G. W. Lampe saw, to 'regard the whole of Scripture as a bundle of oracles, from which any and every expositor can quarry pieces at random to fashion into a mosaic of his own design'.[9] It is a wise rule therefore that we must avoid the deliberate habit of seeking here and there in Scripture for type and anti-type. We have no need to add to the decisive types which bind the New Testament so closely and convincingly to the Old in reinforcing the one Salvation history.

Yet, at times, when one allows one's mind to dwell on the details of Old Testament history, it can be taken up occasionally

[7]   Cf. *The Unity of the Bible*, pp. 95–121.
[8]   *Commentary on Leviticus*, p.2.
[9]   *Typology*, p.36.

by experiences in the lives of individuals which hold the
attention as foreshadowing what was to happen in Christ. Of
course, the most important instances of such correspondence
between what happened in the lives of Old Testament
individuals and in Christ himself are to be found in the two
passages in which he himself found most directly prophetic of
his own sufferings and death. It was in his mind from the
beginning of his ministry that he had to fulfil what was written
in Isaiah 53 and the other servant songs which are obviously
linked up with this one.[10] Moreover as he was facing his
crucifixion his mind dwelt on the twenty second psalm. He
read it as a description of the kind of agony he had to go
through, and he resigned himself to what it described as he
made it his prayer.

The Psalm of course can be historically understood as being
originally the expression of the agony of a righteous servant
of God, possibly David, suffering dreadful persecution at the
hands of the enemies of God. There are certainly such
remarkably coincidental details in the description of what
happened that make us feel that the language written in the
Psalm must have been inspired in some way to be so closely
parallel to the future sufferings of Jesus. Calvin, commenting
on those passages in the Psalm which fit Christ rather than
David himself, expressed the belief that David, at those points,
was inspired by the Spirit to exaggerate the descriptions of his
own sufferings so that they would thus become prophetic

The more remarkable and penetrating description of the
nature of Christ's sufferings in Isaiah 53, we believe, had a
basis and origin similar to that of Psalm 22. In this case the
picture of the sufferer and the sufferings borne, is given in
what seems to be the lament of a community over what they
had done to an innocent victim of wholly unjust community
persecution. They had turned, almost to a man, to godlessness
and licence and the cause of righteousness and truth in their
midst had been upheld by this one outstanding man of God
so unflinching in his witness that he had become the object of
universal hatred. Their resentment against him became so
bitter in its intensity that he was not only ostracised but abused

[10] Isaiah 42:1–4; 49:1–6; 50:4–9; 52:13–53:12.

and put to death. Strangely after his death the memory of his faultless witness and the shame of the suffering they had inflicted on him, had haunted their minds and by the influence of the Spirit of God they had been brought to a repentance that had deeply changed the whole moral and religious outlook of their community. This servant in his witness had thus become a Christ figure. Here, too, we have to recognise the historical typological basis for a poem that under the inspiration of the Spirit is made so truly prophetic of Christ.

When I myself have been preparing sermons or expositions from incidents in the Old Testament I have occasionally been struck by the typological significance of what Foulkes, in his definition, describes as certain 'aspects of the life of an individual'. I refer, for example, to Isaac's willing self-sacrifice of himself in obedience to his father on Mount Moriah, and to the provision of the lamb caught by the horns to be offered as a substitute ('not *your* lamb, Abraham, but *mine!*'). And I have found in the hatred and misunderstanding suffered by youngster Joseph because he was faithful to God in his prophetic witness, a closely typical example of the bitter and deadly hatred incurred by our Lord from those who should have been his brothers. In the story of blameless Jonathan's willingness to be dragged down to complete destruction by his loyal love for his crazy and faithless father I have found an example of Jesus' self-identification with those with whom God has bound him up in the bundle of life. I believe that in having their attention drawn to such typological parallels my congregation have been helped to grasp better than before the marvellous unity given to the Bible by God, and to come to a fuller understanding of important aspects of the Gospel.[12]

---

[11]   In adopting this theory that Old Testaent prophecy arose at times by exaggeration Calvin was following an important school of Church Fathers dominated by Theodore of Mopsuestia who tended in their day to resist the allegorical school of interpretation which closely followed Origen.

[12]   A footnote to the whole chapter:—

We have devoted a distinct chapter to Typology because of the importance which an understanding of it can take in the interpretation of many passages of Scripture, and especially for the light it sheds on the unity of the two Testaments. Since our study of it has involved us in the description and explanation of how there arose within the life of Israel and the Church, a number of inspiring visions of the future, obviously it is the place here to remind the reader of other great Old Testament visions of the future and of how they can have arisen. Indeed some of them did not arise out of the optimistically inspired future hope, which have been the basis of the typological visions we have here discussed. They arose rather, at the very time when those who were inspired to utter them were tending to find themselves in a mood of depression, even brooding in despair. It was, for instance, as Daniel 'continued to watch' after he had been given a depressing vision of the future history of the earth being dominated by a series of kingdoms personified by beasts arising out of the great sea, creating their own turbulence on earth, and each more menacing and brutal than its predecessor, that he was given in contrast his great vision of the coming of 'one like a son of man' coming with the clouds of heaven to rule all nations in justice and peace. (Cf. Dan. 7:13–28.).

The most assuring and comforting vision of the future of the earth or of the individual that any mourner can find in the Old Testament occurs in Isaiah, chapter 25:6–9. It is to be noted that the prophet seems to have been inspired to utter it in reaction to other contemporary oracles, some of them, such as 24:17–20, reflecting utter gloom and despair.

Occasionally, therefore, when the prophets looked to the future they saw it developing, in relation to the present, not by the way we have described as typological. They had no idea of a new age gradually arising on earth out of the development of things as they are. The present state of affairs, they believed, is bound to end in destruction and collapse under the judgment of God. The new age comes as a catastrophic irruption into history, 'inaugurating an entirely new quality of life' (G. E. Ladd). It breaks into history from beyond history on that day (Zech. 9:16) chosen by God, bringing about a new order of things that could not in any way have arisen as an age-long development out of the old, and the vision which the prophet has of it contrasts with anything he could previously have imagined. This kind of vision (as in Zechariah 9:14) is called an apocalyptic vision of the climax of earthly affairs, and the kind of writing in which we find such visions is called 'apocalyptic'.

CHAPTER 11

CENTRAL ISSUES IN INTERPRETATION

Allegory

Towards a Definition

I was once given to review a stimulating and useful book entitled *'Allegory, the Theory of a Symbolic Mode'* which made me feel it was important to deal with this subject other than by the usual warning completely to avoid the use of it in interpreting the Bible. The aim of the book was to make us aware that it was a frequently indulged and healthy habit of the human mind to write texts with an allegorical meaning and in interpreting them to be ready to find an implied allegory. We were given examples of how the works of some popular story tellers of today were perhaps consciously intended by them to convey allegorical meaning. What Angus Fletcher, the author of the book, suggests is certainly confirmed when one listens to discussions on the radio by critics of recent novels. The discussion frequently revolves not around the main surface of the story or in the literary skill evidenced but around what possible other meaning may have been either intended, or was subconsciously latent at perhaps a very deep level, in the mind of the writer. 'The literal surface may make good sense of itself', says Fletcher. 'But sometimes the literal surface suggests a peculiar doubleness of intention, and while it can, as it were, get along without such interpretation, it becomes much richer and more interesting with it'. I have little doubt that the writers of the Bible also in their day sometimes wrote in the way Fletcher has here outlined, with the same allegorical intention, and that they expected their writing to be understood and interpreted as having such an allegorical element.

We do well to begin our discussion on the subject with a reasonable definition of what an allegory is. The best I have found is that 'to allegorize is to say something with the intention at the same time of conveying a meaning other than its literal one', and it follows that to 'interpret a text allegorically is to interpret it in terms of something else'. Picking up on this definition, my friend George S. Hendry in a provocative but trenchant article once wrote: 'I am well aware that a plea for allegorical interpretation will sound strange in this enlightened age. The term has acquired an evil odour. But it is the old story. "Give a dog a bad name." I submit that all public exposition of Scripture is in fact, if not in name, allegorical, for allegorical simply means saying other things, and I have never yet listened to one exposition of any text of Scripture in which the text was not invoked to say other things, and sometimes very other things indeed, from the plain literal sense of the words'.[1]

The Openness of the Bible to Allegory

It has been my experience with the Bible as I worked at its interpretation to discover that more texts than I at first imagined can be understood fully only if they are interpreted in the way which we have just defined. For instance when the writer of the Gospel of Matthew (14:28–33) tells us the story of Peter's zeal to imitate Jesus' walking on the water, and of his terrifying yet triumphant ordeal when his faith lapsed, he was obviously intending not simply to relate a memorable event on the earthly career of Jesus but was intending to remind his future readers that Jesus will never allow zealous souls finally to fail in the boldest ventures that are inspired by his example and call, if they keep their eyes always on himself.

I found quite early in my ministry that when I decided to preach a series of sermons on the miracle stories in the synoptic Gospels, I was helped greatly in interpreting some of these stories (and some of the casual events in Jesus' ministry as well) only when I noticed that they were meant here and there, now

---

[1]   *Scottish Journal of Theology,* Vol. I, p. 46

and then, to be interpreted allegorically. When I began to study them with many of the standard commentaries and biblical works that were then around, and were commonly accepted as standard in the late 1930's, I was not certain that the straightforward exposition of the text would give me the material required adequately to hold the interest of my congregation without finding a considerable amount of 'good sermon illustration' from outside sources. Then, however, I began to read Calvin with his continual hints that even in his gestures Jesus was giving obviously allegorical signs of who he was and what he had come to do — and I thought about Augustine's dangerously true expository hint that 'unless the action is regarded as a figure there is no good in it'.[2] I finally acquired a copy of Trench's *Notes on the Miracles* with all its allegorical illustrations from the Fathers of the early Church. Certainly I found many of these interpretations too forced. Yet it was from this time on, I think, that I began to see that not only the miracle stories, but also much of the Gospel narrative has to be read not simply as once-for-all past history, but also as including important hints of what Jesus Christ, 'the same yesterday, today and for ever', is seeking continually to do for us and say to us in the midst of the Church today as we are gathered in his name. Standing therefore by the definition we have given of 'allegory' we have no hesitation in affirming that there are embedded quite deeply within the evangelical history many passages which, though they have an important and valid literal meaning, can be fully understood only if we resort to a form of allegorical interpretation. I found that this allegorical element becomes especially prominent in what I have come to believe are also reliable historical accounts of Jesus' ministry in the Gospel of John. I have also found it surfacing especially where miracle is described, in some of the stories of the Old Testament. When we consider that so many texts in the Bible are open not only to typological comparison but also to such allegorical treatment, we realise how important it is to enlist the gifts of insight and imagination (Cf. pp. 72ff) in the task of exposition. Moreover we can understand why, when

[2]   *Sermon on the New Testament*, XXVII 7 E T, p. 225.

modern historical methods of interpretation were not thought of, the early Church which leant heavily on allegory as one of its standard methods of interpretation, succeeded so well in understanding the message of the Bible. Here and there in Holy Scripture there are things 'hidden from the wise and prudent' and revealed to those who are willing to depend on the simple use of the imagination. 'The allegorist', writes Blackman, 'stands in defence of the richness of Scripture and of a depth of meaning which he feels, by a kind of spiritual intuition, is not reached by the usual methods of exposition'.[3]

As well as being able to yield the typological and the allegorical comparisons which are so unique to its own special history, the Bible is also of course open to allegorisation on a much more ordinary level. We have to learn to appreciate how often the text is written to convey a compound meaning on a quite mundane level and to be given an allegorical interpretation. When Psalm 121 tells us, 'The sun shall not strike you by day nor the moon by night', or Psalm 91 that 'You will not fear the terror of the night, or the arrow that flies by day, or the pestilence that stalks in darkness', they are deliberately encouraging us to ignore the literal meaning, and to concentrate on the 'saying something else'. In a sermon I once heard on Elijah's experience as a prophet during his isolation by the brook Cherith I found myself impressed, as many others were, by the powerful and skilful way in which the simple 'aside', 'in the process of time the brook dried up', was made the occasion of a series of allegorical warnings and counsels to his over-prosperous hearers not to trust in their wealth or what it could bring. We have to acknowledge that in our interpretation of most of the *Song of Solomon* we are meant continually to rise from the vivid descriptions of the raptures of erotic love either to what is intimate between the human soul and God or to the relation between the Church and Christ. 'We may forgive allegorizing some headaches', writes Grierson, 'inasmuch as it has enabled serious Christians and Protestants to enjoy the *Song of Solomon* without a scruple of conscience, indeed with a sense of positive edification'.[4]

---

[3] E. C. Blackman, *Biblical Interpretation*, p. 176.
[4] *Crosscurrents in 17th Century Literature*, p. 72.

Dangers and Safeguards

Though we ourselves have to be as open to the use of allegory in interpretation of the Scriptures, as they are to its occurrence, we have to be aware of the dangers of its abuse. Whenever allegorizing becomes a method of interpretation and is given any priority in the basic work of interpreting a passage, it nearly always becomes the means by which an irresponsible expositor with no basic training or skill can impose a self-chosen meaning on a text which may have a literal sense far different from that which is finally derived from it.

A recent radio sermon I heard in the United States may be cited as typical. The incident read and discussed was the abortive attempt of Adonijah the son of David to usurp the throne which he knew his father had denied him in favour of Solomon. He nevertheless tried to take advantage of David's irresolution in a conspiracy that would have succeeded had not Nathan the prophet intervened in a timely way to have Solomon hurriedly crowned. The lesson, driven home to the neglect of the many other profound lessons, was that unless each of us speedily settles who is to rule our lives we will have trouble. We all have an Adonijah, or self-will, the usurper which wants to take over. But we can rely on it that God will not eventually allow himself to be cheated of his mastery in our lives and will see to it that the Holy Spirit eventually rules.

The use of allegory as the main method of interpretation, though it often served the Church well in early times, nevertheless enabled it in the Middle Ages, as G. S. Hendry points out, to set itself up as the authoritative interpreter of Scripture. Instead of seeking to find out and subject itself to the Word, it could always decide in advance what any part of Scripture was going to say. Thus through its allegorizing the Church shut itself off from any new truth which a growing rational understanding of the Scripture could bring before it, and there is no doubt that today the use of allegory as a method of interpretation would have the same devastating effect if it were in any way encouraged.

Augustine, whose examples of allegorizing are often cited for the way it should *not* be used,[5] freely admitted that one of the reasons he persisted in its use was that it gave his hearers more pleasure to be taught by allegory than by plain doctrinal proposition. In the passage in the *Song of Songs* in which ewes 'coming up from the washing' are described as 'bearing twins' he finds a reference to the healthy effect of the discipline which the Church imposes on both its clergy and its new members when it strictly separates them from the world. Then he asks why he should spend such time and pain explaining all these detailed allegorical implications when plain teaching could put the same truth across more simply. The reason he gives is that he finds 'more delight indeed' in teaching thus, and his people found 'immense delight' in being taught this way. We have to remember that for Augustine the three conscious aims which all preachers must bear in mind should be to 'teach, delight and move'.[7] His hearers, he believed, would be culturally inclined to respond to the kind of allegorical argument in which he himself was so expert.

We can think of no positive rules which might help anyone to find an allegory in any part of Holy Scripture, but we can suggest some safeguards to prevent the kind of danger we have indicated. Our first observation is that an allegorical interpretation is likely to be desirable and helpful if it arises within the ministry of a pastor or lecturer who is expert in the academic and personal study of the whole Bible. An acceptable allegorical meaning will normally arise in the mind of the

---

[5] The most often quoted example is his interpretation of the Parable of the Good Samaritan: The victim is humanity, the Samaritan is Christ, the inn is the Church, the two pence are the Old and New Testaments.

[6] Cf. Augustine , *De Doct. Christiani* 11.6, on *Song of Solomon* 6:6. We remember how important it was to Luther that the preacher should offend, rather than please (cf. pp.90–91). No contradiction need be implied. It would be a good use of allegory if it could delight the hearer to discover the truth that offends.

[7] The aims of the *orator* as defined by Cicero were, I believe, 'to teach, to *prove* and move'.

interpreter after the basic sense of a passage has been found in the normal way and it is recognised and used and simply for the interest and meaning it can add to what has been already worked out.[8] It will always be one which occurs to us quite spontaneously as or after we submit our minds to the text before us in its literal and historical sense. The mere reading of the text may provoke it. It simply occurs as we turn our attention to what is being said on the ordinary level of discourse. It can seem to leap at us even though we may not be able to explain how we arrived at it. It can never be one which we in any way contrive in our minds and impose on the text.

In spite of all the dangers, we have no doubt however that the writers of the Bible expected their writing at times to be open to the kind of interpretation we have outlined under this heading. It is important that we should not deprive our Biblical exposition of the wealth and depth of meaning and of the human pleasure and interest that can be derived from its legitimate use when the opportunity occurs, and we should be alert to the frequency of such occasions. Allegories 'prove nothing', wrote William Tyndale, 'but the very use of allegories is to declare and open a text, that it may be better perceived

---

[8]   I can think back critically to the early days of my ministry when the genuine meaning of the Old Testament was not well understood. We found it extremely popular with our people if, instead of trying to expound the Old Testament stories, and teaching from them on the context they had in salvation history, we selected some little facet in their superficial structure and simply allegorised freely upon it. How easy it was to let the imagination dwell for the duration of a twenty minute sermon on a text like 1 Kings 20:23, 2 Samuel 18:8, 1 Kings 20:40, Genesis 43:3, etc. I remember reading a sermon by the great Alexander Maclaren on 1 Kings 22:3. Taking it as my text I urged my people to stir themselves up to possess their possessions in Christ, only later to discover the literal context clearly forbade what I had been urging!

and understood. There is not a better, more vehement, or mightier thing to make a man understand than an allegory'.[9]

---

[9] Quoted by A. Bonar, *Op. Cit.*, p.4. I found myself impressed when I heard H. R. Mackintosh preach an almost wholly allegorical sermon on Acts 5:15, likening the shadow of Peter to our possible 'unconscious Christian influence', and another on Exodus 21:5 on the constraining and restricting power of our devotion to Christ.

CHAPTER 12

THE STRUCTURE OF THE BIBLICAL WITNESS

The Need for Openness to Story and Doctrine

I have already touched on the importance of facing the Bible as a whole, and at this point we return to the same theme. Much of what is said in the Bible is in the form of story, or of history told in story. Much is in the form of either direct doctrinal teaching or in ethical instruction derived from that teaching. If we are to allow ourselves to be faced by and subject to the whole of the truth it is there to convey to us, our minds must be continually open to both these quite distinct aspects of its witness. Our purpose in this chapter is to show the importance of allowing the whole Bible its full impact in the interpretation and proclamation of its message.

The Decisive Place of Story in the Service of the Word of God

It is being affirmed emphatically today that the Church has too often in its history allowed the doctrinal aspect of the message of the Bible to dominate its life and thought, and has not seriously enough listened for the Word of God as it is meant to come to us in the form of story. When God revealed himself to us he put much of what he wants to say to us in story. He means it to come home to us today in this latter form and as such he means us to open our minds to it again and again receptively. We need not turn it into doctrine before it can be a powerful event in our thought and life. We must try to understand better than we have done 'the basic narrative quality of human existence'.

In recent years many illuminating studies have appeared which bring out the importance of the part which should be played by story in the formation of the theology of the Church, and much new attention is being presently given to the detailed study of the varied forms taken by the stories of the Old Testament narrative in the belief that these can give us fresh and important insights into the meaning of different texts. 'A true Messianic community', says Moltmann, must be a 'fellowship which narrates the story of Christ, and its own story with that story because its own existence, fellowship and activity spring from that story of liberation. It is a story-telling fellowship which continually wins its own freedom from the stories and myths of the society in which it lives, from the present realisation of the story of Christ.'[1] It is important that our minds should be open to what is being said in this movement. After all the Gospel can be well described as ' the old, old story'. We are taught about both our creation and redemption in the form of story. I find myself sympathetic towards it because I think my own experience can point to two key aspects of the important part which openness to the world of Biblical story can play in the development of Christian life and thought.

I have already spoken of the pervasive influence which came to me as a youngster through having absorbed thoroughly in my mind a whole story world as the Biblical narrative was read continuously to me during the whole length of my school years. In the connection in which I was then writing I referred to it as 'ethical'.[2] The full effect of it, though I was not consciously aware at the time of what was happening, was of a much more all-embracing nature. It shaped my whole understanding of what life was about, determined the value I put on the various things offered me, the constraints that were worth while observing, the rewards that were worth while seeking, and the tragedies that were to be avoided through its restraints. Somehow the Biblical stories held themselves together in my mind as having a divine sanction, and therefore a ring of urgency and closeness to real truth, that I recognised even

[1] *The Church in the Power of the Spirit*, p. 225
[2] See pp.85–88.

then as belonging to no other group of stories from any other culture however noble or religious.[3] It was only later, as I have already described it, that I came more fully to understand what it was about them that gave them this inspiring and constraining preliminary uniqueness in my mind. I was being prepared through them for the issues that matter in the life-struggle that I face today in the salvation history in which I know myself involved in through Christ. By the grace of God my life was even then oriented towards true wisdom and faith. As we all eventually discover, life with God can be full of ambiguities and mysteries. The continual and wide-ranging absorption in Bible-lore enables us marvellously to accept, endure and triumph.

Though I did not realise it at the time, the continual hearing of these 'Bible stories', and the attention I gave them, were also having a further, and even more decisive effect on my mind and morals. They were not only habituating my mind to relate God to every aspect of life, but were moulding an image of God in my mind that was far closer to the truth of the Gospel than could have come to it naturally. (I became such an idealist in my philosophy that I would have adopted an 'ideal' view of God). I find an analogy of what happened to me, in what Johannes Warneck found taking place around him in his work and research on the mission field. The 'teller of the Bible stories discovers that a new religious world is dawning upon the heathen through the simple narration of what God has done for men: that those stories are better fitted than any well thought out address for making blinded idolaters acquainted with the living God: that the simple telling of what God has done in the course of human history makes his image plastic to them and himself no longer a bloodless idea, but an acting, thinking, feeling person. It is the Bible stories that transform the religious thought of the animist'.[4] I can remember my mind

---

[3]   My education had introduced me quite well to the legends of Greece and Rome and even to stories of the Nordic world — and I knew something of those current in Hinduism.

[4]   Quoted by G. E. Phillips, *The Old Testament in the World Church*, p. 112.

being haunted all day by the thought of what a father can feel towards a son when the Headmaster in the morning read at prayers the climax of the story which culminates in David's lament over Absalom, and also when he read about the father in the parable of the Prodigal Son. I am certain such experiences prepared me to respond with faith when I at last heard the deeper meaning of the Cross proclaimed clearly, decisively and doctrinally.

The Decisive Place of Doctrine in the Service of the Word of God

In giving us so much in such a rich world of story and history God has made amply sure that everything he has spoken with such patience and cost to himself will be clearly and fully understood. Continually interlaced with the Old Testament narrative there are explanations of what he is doing. Prophecies are given, lessons are taught and at the heart of the New Testament there are the Apostolic letters. The story by itself is not enough.

I was apt to be greatly moved when, for example, in my teenage days, I heard Paul Robeson singing, 'Were you there when they crucified my Lord?' Yet it was only when I began to understand what it was all about — and it all began with one doctrinal text — that the transforming inner power and of ethical consequences of the history began to unfold in my life. It is so important to have the doctrine alongside the story! Our devotion to Christ can certainly be greatly kindled at a Good Friday service when we hear the passion narratives read and can join in those descriptive hymns which stress the pain of the wounds, the desolation of heart and bring to our mind his cry of abysmal dereliction. Yet how much more powerfully are we moved by those which interweave the doctrine with the story (Wesley!), they enlarge our vision of its meaning and kindle our devotion with a fuller understanding. Peter in his first Epistle was speaking to second or third generation disciples, some of whom seemed to be regretting that they had not had the opportunity of being there and getting to know him as a personal friend. He reminds them that even the Gospel picture they had of him could kindle ardent 'love' of the same kind as any around him in his earthly life had had, and he adds that the further knowledge they now knowledge they now have of the doctrine — of the wonderful things that have come to be revealed *about* him since his resurrection and ascension — can bring us an 'indescribable and glorious joy' which was unknown in its full dimension to those who were his contemporaries in the flesh (1 Pet. 1:8).

There is a place here at this point for my own personal testimony about the enrichment that came in my own Christian experience and ministry when I began to grasp through Calvin's biblical teaching that the preaching of the Word was not merely a means of announcing good news, and that the Lord's Supper was not simply a memorial feast recalling his passion to our minds, but that both together were best understood as means through which we could enter, nourish and live within the saving union with Christ, described both by Jesus himself and Paul as the central mystery of our Christian experience. The recent Alpha courses in a Church with which I was closely connected have proved again, as in many other cases, how powerful the influence of the simplest systematic presentation of 'sound doctrine' within house groups or lay gatherings can become. Through such often basic teaching ordinary members of the community have become articulate about their belief and experience. Mutual prayer and intercession for others have developed within the fellowship, and an urge to evangelism. I personally and continually in my own ministry have found, when challenged to defend the faith or faced by earnest or urgent inquiry, that I was able to cope and sometimes to succeed simply because I had made myself as expert as I could in doctrinal issues. In estimating the place and importance of such issues in the Church we have to remember the liberating and rallying role that doctrinal confessions have played in the struggles it has at times had to go through in order to maintain the integrity of its witness to Christ and to free itself from false leadership.

Of course it is true that our over-emphasis on doctrine to the exclusion of story can bring sterility, and a tendency to divisiveness within the life of the Church, and there have been too many occasions in its history when this has happened. Yet the fear of such happening must not in any way make us put asunder what God has clearly joined together. The part that doctrine continually can play in directing and nourishing the

Church's life, devotion and worship, and enabling it to fulfil its mission must continually be appreciated.

The best analogy I can think of to describe the function which doctrine plays alongside story would be that of a clarifying or crystallising agent enabling what is already there to come to full and clear expression. What more could doctrine say about the Cross that was not already said there and then when it happened — and how otherwise could it have been said? Yet how much more it means when the doctrine is declared and we see it in this new light?

The Need of Each for the Other — Some Practical Issues

Our concern here is to show how important it is that, both in the formation of our theological thought, and in the preparation of the message we have to teach and preach, we should allow our minds to dwell fully on every aspect of the Word of God as it comes to us in both doctrine and story. Too often the Church has hidden important aspects of God's Word from its people (Cf. 1 Sam. 3:17–18). There have been times in Church history when any doctrinal emphasis was regarded with suspicion.[5] More often it has been the doctrinal aspect of the witness of the Bible, confession and catechism that have been allowed too much priority with consequences no less baneful.

I can best convey what I think is helpful on this subject if I illustrate it from the mistake I often made in my early preaching on the Biblical narrative. The natural bent of my mind, inclined to science, has always been towards systematic and rational thinking on any subject. The decisive early encounter I had had on hearing the Word of the Cross gave me a life-long incentive to seek to understand always more fully and clearly what I then saw and heard. Therefore I found my mind at first very fully taken up with the study and discussion of theology, and I tended in my preaching to emphasise doctrine, even

[5]   In the twenties when I was a teenager I heard Browning's line quite often quoted by religious speakers: 'There is more faith in honest doubt, believe me, than in half the creeds'. Christianity was 'life', not 'doctrine'!

when I was preaching on what was story.[6] I tended to expound the passage as if it was there simply to illustrate a series of edifying and challenging doctrines. I had yet to learn that the purpose of the story is much more than that of teaching doctrine. It is there to be told rather than taught. It is indeed impossible to define in any clear way the message a story in the Bible is able to convey as it is read and heard especially within the context of Church worship. As the preacher or teacher before the congregation or Bible- study group goes through a story trying to clarify the details and bring out the meaning, quite other aspects of it than could have been in his or her mind will come home to the hearers or participants. And quite different aspects of the dynamic thrust of the whole story will make their mark. What comes across often when we try to extract doctrines from the story is, as Moberly says, often 'something very much less interesting and memorable than the story itself'. 'It is a feature of the Samuel narratives', says Robert Gordon in his commentary, 'that they often stop short just where we might expect a word of censure or a moralising tailpiece'. We must respect the story as something that will register powerfully in the mind of a hearer in its own way. We do well to remember the protest of the little girl who, listening to her mother's comments on the story they had been reading together, said, 'I would understand it much better Mummy if you wouldn't try to explain it'.

Though the story form of the text must be fully respected as we use it for teaching or proclamation, we have to make sure that it is understood by our hearers as a Bible story. It is meant to be told and received as belonging to the salvation history which God is working out in this world in Christ. In the story as it lies in the Bible there is an intended doctrinal slant which must also be respected. This implies on the part of the teacher or preacher an awareness of the conflict which must take place whenever the Word of God confronts our

[6]   See E. Brunner, *Reason and Revelation*, p.201. 'The Church has had to pay dearly for the fact that it substituted the Christian Catechism for the Biblical history. The revelation of God must be *told,* not *taught.* Where narrative is replaced by doctrine, Greek thought triumphs over the thought of the Bible.'

natural thought world, and seeks to make its impact on things as they are. We are reminded in the New Testament that there are all kinds of doctrines that are, even in the Church, 'strange' (Heb. 13:9) to Holy Scripture. Attempts are quite often made to introduce into the interpretation of the Bible a doctrine entirely foreign to its whole way of thinking and attitude to life. In a milieu where the standard by which all doctrines were tested was the tenets of Freudian psychology, I once heard a sermon in the form of an exposition of the first four chapters of 1 Samuel in which Samuel's severity in his condemnation of Saul and his slaying of the Amalekites, were eloquently attributed to his being forsaken by his mother as an infant, and his strange ex-family fostering by an abnormally minded priest!

While 'sound doctrine' (1 Tim. 1:10, Tit. 2:1) is so necessary and helpful as a guide to interpreting the story it must also be remembered: that it is only in the light of the story that the doctrine itself can be fully understood. For example, the New Testament, when it puts forward ways in which the Cross has to be interpreted, at times isolates, for us to think about, several different aspects of what happened . It speaks of him in one place as showing us the full extent of his love in a heroic saving demonstration. In other places as dying in our place and taking our legal condemnation on himself, or as offering himself instead of us as a ransom price to set us free from all bondage, or as entering into an exchange bargain with us by which, uniting us to himself, he takes on himself all the sin we have done and the death we have deserved, giving us in their place his righteousness, eternal life and goodness. When we think of such analogies justifiably our minds wander to what happens in law courts, in post war settlements and in stock exchanges or bargain basements. Good theological books can indeed be written dwelling on such analogies and casting light on the deep and complex meaning of the atonement.

Such 'doctrine' undoubtedly helps us a great deal as our mind seeks to move towards the truth. Yet we have to turn back even from such sound doctrine again to the 'story'. We have to think of what happens on the Cross as the climax of centuries of the agonizing love and suffering which God so patiently and kindly endured for Israel pleading for them to return and trust him, finding that they even hated him the more, the more he tried. We have to add to this the accounts of the sufferings of the prophets whom he sent as his messengers, especially the one who is described in Isaiah 53, and finally add to this catalogue the fact that knowing all this he sent his dear Son to go through it all again in person — such was his will and his love! When we do so we begin to understand why one of our greatest hymns about the Cross, finally by-passes all doctrine, and tells us simply, 'All the light of sacred story gathers round his head sublime'.

I have quite often found the nature of the love and grace of God deeply and touchingly implied here and there in the Old Testament story in a quite indirect way, without his even being mentioned. I refer to the immensely tender and intense sympathy with which the Biblical writers describe the suffering of the quite innocent victims of the cruelest human tragedy, not their own fault. We find this, for example, in the stories they tell, of what Phinehas' widow (1 Sam.4: 19,20), Jeroboam's wife (1 Kings 14:1–17) and Rizpah[7], Saul's concubine, (2 Sam. 21:7–10) had to go through simply because they were linked up with some of the tragic failures of those who ruled Israel. How did the writers get their sensitivity if not from their close fellowship with the God who was there inspiring them with the human interest and tragic sympathy with which they were writing? Obviously when God was compelled to set in motion his judgments he wants us to know that he cared intensely about such helpless, then insignificant, individuals who were caught up and dragged down under what was taking place.

At this point, by the way, it is worth while pointing out how important it is that the word 'love' in the doctrine 'God is love' is to be interpreted in the light of the whole story about God given in the Old and New Testaments, and certainly not in the way 'love' is used, often erotically, in our media and common conversation. We need continually to remember the Apostles' directive, 'In this is love .... that he loved us, and sent his Son...' (1 John 4:19). All our Biblical doctrines indeed, are meant to

---

[7]   Tennyson was moved to write what Herbert Grierson, my English teacher, regarded as one of his greatest poems, by the story of Rizpah.

be understood similarly in the light cast on them by the whole Biblical story. I have found this rule specially helpful when I have had to think over how God exercises his sovereignty in predestination. The Bible everywhere clearly and emphatically teaches that we are saved by pure grace by a love that loved us before we were born. He loved and chose us from all eternity to be his. But we do not find in the New Testament, however, the unambiguous expression which we would logically expect of the contrasting doctrine — that God from the very beginning makes a decision to reject, or even to pass by, those who finally decide to respond to him. We find it, rather, implied in one or two Old Testament stories, (those of Esau and Saul, and of the house of Eli, for example), that God can originally set his choice on people whom he has finally to reject, as they reject him.[8] I find myself therefore unable to accept that God from all eternity would elect 'some to damnation' in the same way as he elects 'some to salvation'. We have continually to beware lest our thought of God, and what he does becomes dominated by received doctrine rather than by Biblical story.

When I finally realised how important it was in preaching to allow the story which I had as my text to make its full impact on my hearers I found I had to modify greatly the structure of my sermons. For a long time I cast what I had to say on a text in the thematic structure which began to prevail in the Church in the middle ages, in which there is an attempt to have an introduction and conclusion and a thematic unity and several clear doctrinal heads that people could remember. When my text was a story, however, I began to find it better often to follow the homiletic structure of the sermon, so often used in the early Church fathers. Beginning (with no need for any introduction) with the first verse of the passage, simply moving through the happenings of the text in the order of their occurrence and finishing where the story finishes trying to allow the story itself to make its impact along with my comments.

[8] The case of Judas I regard as unique and exceptional, and I do not find Paul's discussion in Romans, chapter 9, directly applicable to the specific point under discussion.

It is worth while mentioning at this point that in thus aligning my preaching so closely to the content and movement of the Biblical stories, I found myself no longer in need to find any of the 'illustrations' from outside sources which I had found necessary to make doctrinal preaching 'relevant' to life. Frequent, varied and marvellously relevant analogies to our personal, church and wider social life come before us as we move through the story world presented to us in the Bible. The relevance indeed time and again intrudes itself into our minds without our seeking to find it, and we have no difficulty in applying it. J. Blaikie in his *Preaching and Preachers in Scotland* speaks of how Thomas Halyburton was able 'to associate every feeling, good or bad, with some text of Scripture which he duly set down; for he firmly believed that every winding of his subtle heart, every refuge of lies to which he had fled, every art and artifice of Satan with which he had been plied was mirrored in the Word of God'.[9] We ourselves could add from our experience. I would personally make his list include all the intimate and complicated problems that can arise within family life and marriage, all our internal Church problems and conflicts, and most of the economic and social issues that have to be faced if justice is to be done for all and God's will is to prevail in social life, and if nation is to live alongside nation without potential warfare.

Story *and* Doctrine! If we are to become truly 'rooted and built up' in Christ (Col. 2:7) we need each in its place alongside the other, fulfilling its particular task. We can think of it aptly as being the story which *roots* us in him and the doctrine which *builds us up* together in the faith.

[9]   p. 248.

CHAPTER 13

THE INTEGRITY OF THE BIBLICAL WITNESS

The Centrality and Reliability of History within the
Biblical Narrative

We now must remind ourselves that when we are speaking of
'story' in the Bible we are speaking mainly about history and
referring to events of historical importance. Certainly as we read
the Bible we find it difficult to grasp and remember that we are
reading an actual history book. The centuries of difference
between us and the 'ancient world' it talks about is so great that
we are apt to think of many of the accounts of what then happened
as simply myth or legend. Much of the narrative has the shape of
'story' told possibly to teach lessons about life and providence, or
perhaps to entertain as well. Moreover, the outcome of events
seems to depend so often on quite wonderful miracles of the
kind that simply don't happen in our present day 'historical world'!

Yet the Bible is given to be accepted by us as a history. Even
when the story is so full of meaning, as carefully and cunningly
constructed and told so beautifully, as is the story of Joseph
and his brothers, it is history. Even when we are told of the
'unbelievable' miracle of the crossing of the Red Sea, of the
marvellous conception by a virgin of a man child, of the rising
of Jesus from the grave so that the tomb was empty, we are
meant to understand that we are being told history. The stories
of the Bible are handed down to us with the primary purpose
of bearing witness to what God was doing and saying in working
out his purpose in the history both of his people and of the
world. Most of them can be fully appreciated only if they are
received and understood as having happened to further this
purpose, and our primary concern in interpreting them should
be to find out and weigh up what they have to say to us as
historical documents.

Of course the telling of deliberately contrived 'stories' occurs within the history. The parables of Jesus cannot be called 'history', though they were told with an important historical purpose in mind, and there are parables also in the Old Testament. There is the book of Job which can be edifyingly read and studied whether it is regarded as fiction or history. Having recently moved home and Church twice I have listened to two quite different expositions of the Book of Jonah, both by sincere evangelical pastors. The first took it as pure story — a tract designed to re-kindle the missionary zeal of God's people. The second took it as an account of historical fact. Reviewing them I have felt that the exposition of the book as a story was both more effective and truer to the purpose for which the book was originally inspired. I have already made it clear how powerfully the first chapters of Genesis have impressed me as meant to be regarded mainly as consisting of story. The Bible stories will come home to us all at different times under different circumstances in different ways. There are places where the narrator, even when giving what he intends to be accepted as factual, also in telling the story gives it allegorical touches of which we are meant to take notice in our exposition, when we interpret the narrative portions of the Bible. We have to ask ourselves if the writer of the passage in front of us had in his mind such other purposes than to be purely historical in his witness.

From the time I began to read and study the Bible seriously, I found myself inclined to believe that where the witness was clearly historical, I was being told what happened with sufficient clarity and truth so that I could accept the facts before me as reliable enough to help me to understand what God was both saying and doing in the events recorded. This inclination of mind I took to be what Calvin was referring to in his teaching about the 'testimony of the Holy Spirit' to the Holy Scriptures as the Word of God.[1] In my case, and I believe it was the same as Calvin's, it was a testimony not simply to the message of the Scriptures but also to the facts recorded. We are not being led astray when we accept the historical witness as genuine.

[1]   Cf. pp.6. John 14:2. ('If it were not so, would I have told you?'), can be applied here.

It is obvious that where the witness of the writer is to what is historical we cannot seek the closeness to fact or accuracy in detail which we would expect or look for in a modern history book. Even while giving a witness that was under God's control and adequately served his purpose, I believe they were given freedom to be themselves — and some of them were certainly more cut out to be story tellers than historians. In the service they gave to God they were able to add touches in their own style to their account of an 'incident'. As we read their work we can justly imagine them embellishing an occasional feature and exaggerating the numbers involved for what they believed to be the glory of God. Yet we can believe firmly that God's concern for the truth of his Word would ensure that they understood what he wanted them to write and that he would constrain their obedience so that what they wrote could take its place within the book designed by him to be consistently genuine in its witness to truth and set apart to have a special place and purpose in the life of Israel his people and the Church[2] which he had for centuries designed it to take. God so controlled their testimony that it would not bring his Word into disrepute.

Facing the Miraculous Element in the Biblical Narrative

The question whether we believe the Bible to be historically reliable or not will involve how far we are prepared to believe its miracles took place. It is therefore important that we should take time briefly to review the extent and nature of the miraculous element within the Bible narrative.

When we discussed the extraordinary transformation of custom and outlook which God gradually brought about in the life of Israel throughout the centuries we found ourselves impelled to call it a 'miracle'. All that he accomplished working providentially and unobtrusively in this long drawn out process over centuries in the realm of thought and the formation of human character, and truly oriented devotion to himself is

[2] The Bible is aptly called 'Holy' because God has separated it from all other literature for this quite special use in the fulfilment of his purpose.

miraculous. We know from the New Testament what was in God's mind and purpose as he worked so patiently and wonderfully with Israel. He is making history move towards the occurrence of one great final miracle — the transformation of all human life through the incarnation, life, death and resurrection of Jesus Christ.

This background of determined purpose and marvellous progress has to be remembered when we think of why and how the unique events of the Old Testament, which we call 'miracles' took place. Since God is so graciously near to Israel in the midst of this unique salvation history, so close in his presence, so great in his power, so pledged to overcome all evil, so strong in his purpose that such things as the crossing of the Red Sea and the falling of fire from heaven at Carmel, had to take place. God is doing merely what had to be done if history is to move in his way. We have to remember that for the Old Testament prophets the most sheerly miraculous aspect of what was happening to them throughout their history was that God in choosing them in the first place, should have overlooked all the potential wickedness and then should have patiently held on to them by faithfully forgiving their sins. This hidden miracle of forgiving love was always in their minds when they thought clearly and truly about God, and in their praise of him and their expressions of the wonder of his doings they gave this first place.[3]

When Jesus came he picked up this latter aspect of God's miraculous Old Testament work of reconciling the world to himself. God had marvellously dealt with everything hurtful and fateful that had damaged his relationship with humankind and was seeking in the same unbelievably gracious way to call them back to himself! When his birth was announced by the angels it contained the good news that men and women everywhere were now in a position to find 'peace on earth' with God. He went about continually offering the forgiveness

---

[3]   This aspect of the message of the Old Testament is brought out most clearly and strikingly by H. R. Mackintosh in *The Christian Experience of Forgiveness* He dwells on, e.g., Exod: 32:30ff; Micah 7:18; Isa. 44:22–24.

of sin to all who would have it — an offer that was made possible then and for ever because he was to die on the Cross and rise again. Of course, even during his life on earth his Word of forgiveness and reconciliation proved itself effective. Time and again it happened that those around him who came under the compelling influence of his person and voice ceased to hide themselves from him and his holiness, and opened their lives fully to his transforming influence. It was those whose faithfulness to him endured while the whole world turned against him, and they formed the nucleus of those to whom he could appear and commission to be his Church after his resurrection.

Alongside this pure miracle of reconciliation Jesus also preached a word of redemption that was accompanied by even more spectacular miracles than had ever before occurred at any period of Old Testament history. He preached redemption. 'The kingdom of God is at hand', he said, and as he did so he healed people of sicknesses, cast out the devils that so grievously disturbed their social and home life, and even raised the dead. He wanted it known that he had come to make possible his new future age on earth — the 'kingdom of God' he called it, an era of salvation, bringing redemption from all the evil things that had blighted life on earth. He spoke of himself as the 'stronger one'[4] who had come to disturb and cast out the 'strong man' who had been allowed to reign too long on earth in peace.. He claimed indeed that his own presence and his power to do these miracles were to be read as signs that this glorious future age would indeed very soon break finally into human history and bring about its long hoped for consummation. 'It was by the finger of God', he claimed, that he was able to cast out demons and his ability to do such miracles was a sign that 'the kingdom of God has come upon you' (Luke 11: 20).

William Manson my New Testament teacher asked us once to notice the earliest description of Jesus as a man given by Peter when he was preaching about him. He dwelt not on the

---

[4] Luke 11:21–22. Cf. Isa. 49:24. Notice how Jesus at times could utter rebuke, e.g., to the fever (Luke 4:39) and to the wind (Matt 8:26).

divine truth of Jesus' teaching, nor on the transcendental greatness and quality of his person but rather on 'the prolific number and extraordinary nature of the miracles he had done especially in Galilee (Acts 2:22, 10:38). Obviously, as the Apostles began to look back on who he was and what he had come to do, these works were like 'a halo of divine signs', around him, and 'authenticating him to Israel as the deliverer sent by God'.

As we read through the Book of Acts we find that the Apostles, like Jesus himself, made it their first concern in their ministry to preach the forgiveness of sins through his death and resurrection, to bring about the reconciliation of men and women with God. When Jesus made the promise to them in the upper room that they would do 'greater miracles' than he himself (John 14:22) we believe that he was referring to the innumerable multitudes who would undergo miraculous moral transformation through their proclamation of forgiveness. Yet with such priority always in their minds, they did not neglect also to preach redemption and to seek evidence of its imminence. The outpouring of the Spirit on the Church at Pentecost was regarded by them as a sign confirming to them that the 'last days'[5] had indeed come upon them and that they themselves were living under the pressure of the new age of which Jesus had often spoken. They could expect to find happening around them, as they preached reconciliation, also the same miraculous signs of the coming redemption as accompanied Jesus' own proclamation. They were therefore always on the alert to find the same kind of 'miracle' happening and at times prayed for such.

From all that has been said we can derive some guidance about how we should think both about the natural world we live in and the possibility of miracles occurring within it. 'Science' too often dominates our common way of thinking about the universe and the course of our lives. God is thought of as controlling all events from a distance by rigid natural laws. A miracle, if it took place, would have to involve the

[5]   Richardson. Cf. in *The Miracle Stories of the Gospels,* p.40. Speaking of Pentecost as a sign of the last days, he refers to Joel 2:28, Isa. 44:3, Ezek. 11:19, Zech. 12:10.

violation of things as they are and should be a quite strange, even 'impossible' event! The Bible, however, demands a quite different line of thought. The miracles of the Bible, as Emil Brunner said, are to be thought of as 'aspects of the one great miracle to which the whole Bible witnesses', and 'signs that the Creator himself has broken through the creaturely barrier'. They are to be thought of as simply special and indeed wonderful examples of the same marvellous providential care as was already and always being lavished by God in the life of his people throughout the course of salvation history. All the works of God recorded in the Bible history are wonderful, yet, as Wheeler Robinson puts it, 'at particular points of time and space the wonder of what is happening is intensified'. 'A miracle', says Dibelius, 'is an event in which the hand of God, which is always there, can be more clearly traced than at other times'. Miracles dramatically reveal an activity which is continually taking place. H. R. Mackintosh defined miracle as 'any event which forces us to say: "This is the Lord's doing and it is marvellous in our eyes"' (Psalm 118:23).

It can be specially helpful to follow the hint Jesus himself gave us when he spoke about miracles as being the invasion of this world's life by the 'kingdom of God'. We are to think of miracles as happening because this world has been already invaded as R. Eucken suggests, by a 'new order of reality'[7] with other powers than we ourselves can naturally think of from an ordinary human experience. As C. S. Lewis puts it: 'It is inaccurate to describe miracle as something that breaks the laws of nature. It doesn't …. The divine act of miracle is not an act of suspending the pattern to which events conform, but of feeding new events into that pattern.'[8] Moreover we must realise that the events we are thinking and speaking about here as miracles are quite unlike any other unusual or extraordinary happening that might occur anywhere in human life, in that

---

[6]   In *Gospel Criticism and Christology,* pp. 83–84.

[7]   J. N. Figgis, *Civilisation at the Crossroads,* pp. 163–5, gives the quotation I have made from R. Eucken, in *Christianity and the New Idealism,* and is worth reading for his own comments.

[8]   C. S. Lewis, *Miracles,* p.72

they are simply aspects of the good news, 'the teaching and proclamation and therefore the existence of the man Jesus'.[9]

Points of Tension and Growing Assurance

It will be obvious of course that the use of the word 'reliability' to define the standard that we are to expect to find in the Bible leaves room within the Church for wide differences of opinion about what the Bible affirms and teaches. This wide difference is also due to the nature of the Bible itself. God has chosen to speak his word through what is a varied collection of books written under human as well as divine pressure and inspiration. Moreover, we ourselves are free to attach our own personal doubts or certainties at times to many different aspects of the texts as we interpret them.

Apart from the acceptance of the view that the Bible is inerrant in all that it says, even those who tend to take a conservative attitude towards it can reach only a vague consensus about where and how to draw the line they think important. I have never been much impressed by 'proofs' that 'the Bible is true', though I have read the literature published under this heading. I have visited archaeological sites in Palestine and have seen convincing evidence of its accuracy here and there. I hope, however, that a short account of my own experience can be helpful to those who have travelled, or are possibly willing to travel on a way similar to my own.

Early in my ministry when I was preparing my sermons and expositions I found myself frequently in tension and at times profound disagreement with the then up-to-date standard critical commentaries which I was able to consult. I believed that the Biblical witnesses in their day had in their own way and in their life-situation been encountered by the same Word of God as I myself had heard and understood in Christ. It was my task to seek to discover the relevance for us within the Church today of what had happened to them there and then, under the Word of God, and through their witness to enable the people in my pews to understand and listen again to that Word. Yet when I read most of the contemporary commentaries, I found that the great majority of the scholars whom I consulted

[9]   Cf. Karl Barth, *Church Dogmatics*, *IV/2 p. 215.*

did not share my aims, and would not have understood the questions I was asking of the texts. They did not seem to be primarily concerned to find out from the study of the text what God was working out in the furtherance of salvation history. Instead, most of the information I was given about the text seemed to be only of an antiquarian value, and many of their comments, had I passed them on to my people, would have brought confusion and contradiction instead of the edifying and challenging word I myself had hoped to preach.

Fortunately my task was simply to teach and preach as faithfully as I could what I heard from the text, and I did not need to enter controversy. I tried to use what I found helpful but I often had to reject what I read, especially the quite frequent suggestions that the historians could at times have invented any highly important happening, or that an editor could have concealed important aspects of an incident, or distorted the God-ordained trend of events to suit some purpose of his own. I had a feeling at times that I was listening to the voice of 'a stranger' (John 10:5). It was over the interpretation of the Patriarchal stories that I found myself, soon after I began my theological training in acute opposition to what was held out to be accepted. I had already formed a strong conviction that these narratives could be understood as having a good historical basis. I had found an enlightening and encouraging similarity between the records of what Abraham and Jacob went through under the Word of God and my own Christian experience, and I was convinced that at least the narrative genuinely described real people. The critical views at the time, however, made them pure inventions dating about the time of the Hebrew monarchy, and perhaps the product of folklore, possible invented to justify Israel's claim that since they had originally dwelt in the land they could now justly dispossess all later claimants as the intruders.

My experience with the Bible has gradually taught me how important it is to keep continually and reverently in mind what I originally came to believe about the purpose and holy use for which God had inspired and ordained it. I have found that as I have been able to hold on to what I found it clearly saying to me through all the tensions and difficulties that have arisen through my doing so, that I have been confirmed in my convictions and often found them to be clarified.

I have been helped by the fact that till at least the 1960's the theological climate within the Church began to change greatly through a new appreciation of the teaching of the Reformation. The many studies in Biblical theology which appeared began to become more truly Biblical. Archaeological findings and other research studies tended to show that the Bible, in its accounts of ancient history, was more accurate that had been previously thought. I profited also by being able with my slight smattering of German, to read the Biblical expositions that were being given in the pulpits of Switzerland and Germany. These encouraged me to by-pass the critical restraints that had hitherto discouraged me from preaching directly and seriously from the Biblical narrative as it stands in the text. I eventually found the critical climate in Old Testament studies so greatly altered that I was able to find acceptance by responsible reviewers, and grateful readers, for two books of studies in the Patriarchal narratives.

When it came to deciding on 'reliability' in connection with the miracle stories of the Bible I found myself in tension not only with the critical commentaries of the time but also with my own foolish 'slowness to believe; (Cf. Luke 24:25). Even keeping in mind the warning of Rawlinson that 'no wise person will proceed rashly to draw limits between what is and what is not possible'[10] I allowed in the reporting of these incidents too broad a margin of liberty to the enthusiasm and didactic aim of the Biblical writer. I have to admit that I shared something of the prevalent suspicion in the Church over at least some of these stories. Many of the most sincere Christians I knew were firm in their acceptance that the Bible was a book that pointed them to Christ, told them how the world was prepared to receive and understand what he said and did. They accepted too that he could have healed people's sickness by inspiring them with faith. Yet when it came to such stories as the turning of the water into wine and the feeding of the multitudes, they had to be given entirely secular explanations

[10]   In his *St. Mark*, p.40

of how they might have happened. Preachers like Leslie Weatherhead relieved them of any tension by offering purely psychological explanations of such incidents. I myself, moreover, was inclined at this time to believe the theory that the Gospel of John was designedly composed to make Christianity acceptable to Greek readers and I thought its miracles might be contrived stories. I must admit that when it came to the coin in the fish's mouth, not to mention some of the Elisha stories, I was inclined to pray at times: 'Lord, I believe, help thou mine unbelief'.

I found that the nature of the miracle stories themselves gave me a profitable way of interpreting them which enabled me for some time to evade deciding how far I believed the accounts of them to be historically factual. It is in place here to refer to an important feature of the Biblical miracles which did not require to be mentioned in the previous section. I quote: 'In assessing the meaning of the miracle stories we must always take into account their purpose and spiritual value. God has used miracles to teach truths about himself, his nature and purposes which he could express in no other way'.

Since so many miracle stories could be profitably expounded by concentrating simply on the truths they taught about God and the life of faith, I found myself therefore inclined when I expounded them to evade the issue of factuality.[11] I found of course that my congregations were readily willing to listen and profit from the many allegorical interpretations of the miracle stories of the Gospels, especially if they were given the impression that the factuality of the story did not matter. It was at this point that I discovered the rich wealth of meaning that could be derived from the stories about the work of Elijah and Elisha. I found them appealing greatly to the imagination, full of fascinating analogies and allegorical touches. When I found myself invited to speak at conferences I centred my teaching on them and found them so acceptably received that I published a book *Elijah and Elisha* for which there were several demands for reprint.

[11] W. Neil in his *Cambridge History of the Bible* points out that Thomas Woolston in 1727 advocated the allegorical interpretation of the miracles because 'no reasonable person could believe them possible'!

I learned eventually however, what I regard as a most important lesson: that when I stopped the practice of taking 'spiritual' or allegorical lessons from some of the Biblical incidents which presented difficulties to my natural way of thinking, and took them seriously as fact, I began to find a deeper and sometimes a different meaning in them as I more fully discovered their factual significance. This was especially brought home to me when I was asked to write continuous studies in I and II Kings. I made the important discovery that the whole section about Elisha was seriously written to show how, throughout his long career, he gradually became a growingly important spiritual and political influence at the most important later stage of the struggle between Baalism and Yahwism that had been so decisively begun by Elijah at Carmel. I found that approaching the stories with this in mind enriched greatly the meaning I was able to find in many of them and I have been able to appreciate and, I think, to point out the unique and penetrating insight which it was in the mind of the writer of the history to illustrate in his account.

It is as we probe and trust it that the Word proves its own integrity. The more positive my approach has been to any text or narrative that I found difficult either to accept or expound, the more justified I have found myself in having taken it. It was as I gradually and systematically worked my way through more and more books of the Bible, often discovering helpful and enlightening meaning in passages that I had previously regarded as either most difficult to accept or as of only peripheral importance, that I became more and more convinced of the inspiration of the text, and the reliability of what they were seeking both to report and to teach. In the narrative passages it was as I began to take the report as reliably factual that I found a deeper meaning which confirmed the truth of the account of the incident.

I can illustrate further the point I am making from my experience in expounding the miracle stories I have mentioned. It was only when I placed myself as having to preach on the coin in the fish's mouth, that my first thoughts about it, as I tried to find a reason for it, became positive. The more I continued to think over the meaning of the incident, and the purpose that could have lain behind it, the more deeply I was struck by the unsearchable wisdom of the mind that lay behind it, and the more convinced I became that no human story teller could have devised such a tale to foist either on Jesus or on the readers of the Gospel.[12] I had much the same kind of experience when I set myself to preach a series on the seven signs and on the discourses in John's Gospel. I found it finally impossible to take the Gospel as written by an inspired disciple to make the person, teaching and life of Jesus acceptable to the Greek way of thought that was so prevalent in the growing Church. I began to see that it was by the intention of Jesus himself that what took place at Cana of Galilee was in fact laden with profound allegorical meaning, and I have become convinced that John's Gospel of the three years' ministry of Jesus, punctuated by several visits to Jerusalem, gives a reliable outline of what actually happened.[13]

I have found it a help in my own Christian life, as well as in my theology, prayer and preaching to have this growing assurance of the truth of the Word of God and I am certain that there are many around within our congregations who would be greatly helped if they could share it! The Bible is too often hindered from making its full and enriching impact on the minds and lives of our lay people, because after many years they have been led to share the current doubts amongst pastors and scholars about the reliability of its witness. Though our Christian faith does not rest on the Bible but on Christ who speaks and gives himself through it, the Bible itself remains the means through which he is waiting and seeking to give them that extra vision, stability and continuing assurance that are too often being sought by some in ways that are much less helpful. I believe that some measure of the decline facing us in Church can be put down to what P.T. Forsyth diagnosed as our lack of 'Positive Preaching'. Years ago, at a ministers' 'fraternal' in a district of Glasgow, the Pastor of our largest congregation, when he heard I had been preaching the previous Sunday on one of Jesus' miracles, remarked that he himself could never preach about miracles. If he did so, he said,

[12] See my Gospel Mira*cles,* p. 132 ff.
[13] See The Gospel *of John,* Introduction, p.xv ff.

'my people would leave the Church'. I had no answer at that moment, but later on I realised the question I should have asked: How could he or any one else tell that that was the case, until the miracle was first preached on and they had a chance to reject or accept what it taught about Christ, and offered the hearer? (Cf. Rom. 10:17).

As Pastors we must not leave our people unchallenged in their doubts about the Word of God. Though we cannot satisfactorily prove its reliability we can at least seek to uncover its meaning. 'Blessed is anyone', said Jesus, 'who takes no offence at me' (Matt. 11:6). Jesus is here referring to those things in the account of his ministry and teaching which might tend to raise difficulty or perplexity in the minds of those who hear about him (i.e. to 'offend'). We can take encouragement from the implied promise. As we seek to lead our people through those passages in the Gospel story that might at first offend or perplex them, and help them to discover meaning in what at first raised opposition in their minds, the blessing Jesus promised will follow. We need to cease being nervous or apologetic in our approach to people with the Word. One of the many memorable and wise exhortations of my revered teacher H. R. Mackintosh was: 'Preach to faith and you will get faith!'

Appendix — Towards the Awareness and Recovery of Miracle today

The description we have given of how Christ was at work through the Apostles in the New Testament Church should lead us to expect to find in our Church today the same miraculous element powerfully present, especially evidencing itself in the preaching of the Word and the faithful celebration of the Sacraments. It should also encourage us to hope that his presence in such a marvellous reconciling work also means that he is as anxious today as he was then to answer the prayers that are also raised at the same time in our midst for physical healing. Unfortunately among some of the main line Reformed Churches, in one of which I myself was nurtured, there has been and still is a reluctance to recognise that the powerful preaching of the Word of the Gospel should, as it did in Apostolic days, involve in its wake anything comparable to the healings of a remarkable nature which then took place.

The leaders of the Church at the time of the renewal and reformation of the Church in the sixteenth century gave traditional and well-considered reasons for discouraging the expectation we have been describing. At the height of the movement the minds of men and women became occupied almost wholly with the quite marvellous spiritual and reconciling aspects of what the Gospel had brought into their lives in a transforming way. They were forgiven. They had a new insight into the Word and the grasp it gave them of Christ by faith. They were united to him, had peace and communion with God, fellowship one with another and the hope of glory — all this was one astonishing miracle! Certainly in the wake of this whole movement prayer became real and it was believed it was answered by God. But such prayer within the Church community was not then in any way systematically directed towards a continuous ministry of healing of which people could avail themselves. The view prevailed that the miraculous healings which had been prominent within the Apostolic Church had continued only for a limited time. They had remained a feature of the Church's life only as long as they were needed to add their convincing witness to the Gospel while it was gaining ground. From the time when the Church was firmly established in the world, however, it was God's will that such miraculous happenings should cease to have any prominence.[14] God intended the Church finally to grow retaining simply as the heart and inspiration of its whole life what came to it directly through the Word and Sacraments as Christ had ordained them.

The subsequent history of the Church seems to have proved that it was a serious mistake for it ever to try in this way to limit the sphere or effectiveness of the Word of God over any aspect of the human need facing it. Gradually and sadly over the years attempts to draw too strict a dividing line between inward forgiveness and physical healing took its toll, and the Church in its strange unbiblical fear of courting and harbouring too much of the 'supernatural' began to lose all trace of it in its thought life and work. My experience in the ministry during the late thirties and the second world war was that even the

---

[14] See Calvin, Comm on Mark 16:17, Matt: 24:24.

Word and Sacraments had by gradual usage become bereft of all mystery and miracle. Preaching was thought of as an activity on a wholly human level, and the Sacraments as mere speaking symbols. Personal prayer was practised mainly as a means of self-expression and spiritual development. Certainly common prayer was held to be of good social use and there was still left to us some mystical hope that as we gathered together in his name Christ would give 'his presence' in our midst and we would sense it.

I was grateful at that stage in my ministry to read the concern expressed over this development by two theologians whom I found helpful — Emil Brunner and D. S. Cairns.[15] Both traced the beginning of the Church's malaise back much earlier than I myself have so far indicated. For Brunner, it began when the Church became established under Constantine and Theodosius when it 'failed to have the courage to proclaim the miraculous implications of the unity of the Word and action of God which is the distinctive element in Biblical Revelation'. Cairn's accusation was similar: 'No matter what date we choose for that momentous cessation, whether the fifth century or the close of the New Testament Canon', he writes, 'the root idea always is that miracles are dangerous, a kind of heavenly explosive that may wreck the safe established order .... the miracles of the Spirit gradually ceased, because by compromise with the world the Church got out of touch with the pure grace of God'. The title of Cairns' book was *The Faith that Rebels*. A true faith, he asserted, that followed the way of Jesus would never seek to accept or resign itself to things like disease which were obviously contrary to God's will. It would always tend to break out into prayer and action that obviously signified rebellion against their presence and would seek and expect, as he did, God's help in their banishment from the earth, with a faith like his, exercised in his name.

Though the Church today here and there in the West may have lost popularity and status, and is revealing serious division in its ranks over newly emerging moral issues, nevertheless many of us have found taking place in its life and thought one

[15] See Emil Brunner, *Reason and Revelation,* p. 164 and D. S. Cairns, *The Faith that Rebels,* pp. 31–32.

very heartening development. Many of its theologians, pastors and lay-leaders have for the past generation been realising in a way not grasped so firmly for centuries, that it is of the essential nature of a true Church to give its witness and do its work as a community which lives always on the verge of miracle, and the discovery is being made that the Church of today by the will of God continues indeed to be the unique sphere on earth by which Salvation history moves towards its consummation when Christ will come again, He introduces into our life at times, even now, some foretaste or pledge of the glory which will come upon us in its fullness at the last day. We are meant to find that the living Word which dominates our life together within this movement has not been deprived of the same authority and power to work its will which it had when he himself was present in the flesh on earth to speak it.

While no one factor can be pin-pointed as giving us the key towards the full recovery we must seek in this matter, we can encourage and assure ourselves greatly from the words Jesus himself spoke in the upper room before he left his disciples. He spoke of how his going to the Father (by way of his Cross, resurrection and ascension) was going to open up for them a quite new opportunity of effective praying such as they had never before been able to take (Cf. John 14:12–14 and 16:23–24). Now through such praying 'in his name', they were going to make it possible for even miracles of the kind he himself had done to happen in the world around them. 'The one who believes in me will do the works that I do, and greater works that these' (14:12). We have already interpreted the adjective 'greater' to refer to the prolific number of miracles that would happen as the Church spread. We cannot help interpreting the central promise in his words, however, as a pledge that prayer in his name would now bring about even the kind of physical healing he himself had done. Moreover we cannot help hearing these words as directly addressed to us today as they were to the disciples then. Here we are promised that as the course of history moves on to its goal in Christ and directed by God, he will be ever ready to find space within it for answers to the prayers that arise from us to him, 'in the name of Jesus'. God indeed is himself seeking to break miraculously out of the course history might have taken by ever-new departures in answers to such prayers. This is why throughout all the Gospels, but especially in these last words, there are so many challenges to us to ask with confidence, even boldness (Cf. John 14:13–14, 15:7, 16:24).

It is a healthy development therefore within the life of the Church that a place is being found for regular services of intercessory prayer for healing. It can certainly be a helpful symbol of impulsive sympathy for those who pray for the sick to lay hands on them. Moreover we have to be thankful that within the Church fellowship there are those who are given the special gift of healing (1 Cor. 9: 12 and 30), and who administer healing this way beneficially sometimes to a wide Church public.

While we seek an adequate place for a healing ministry within the Church, we at the same time have to concede that it must be kept quite distinct from and subordinate to the Church's central 'ministry of reconciliation' (1 Cor. 5:18). The pastor within the Church must have it as the chief concern in the name of Christ to offer forgiveness and new life here and now to those who will believe the Word and receive him by faith — all this quite apart from and before any other kind of healing is in question.[16] The pastor can through Word and Sacrament offer and indeed give such blessings with a confidence which it would be presumptuous to assume in relation to any action aimed at bringing healing to the body — even the laying on of hands. Yet it is God's will that while we do these things we should not leave the other undone (Cf. Matt. 23:23).

It is worthwhile, in closing, to remember that life within the New Testament Church was characterised by miracle not only in the realms of reconciliation and of redemption, but also in that of providence. The New Testament shows us God actively answering the prayers of his people and responding to their trust in every kind of need, at times for protection from injury and injustice, deliverance from prison or persecution, guidance

---

[16]   To quote H. R. Mackintosh again: 'If we find ourselves forgiven, we are confronted by sheer miracle right at the centre of our life. Forgiveness is the verifying experience of the supernatural.'

in planning and perplexity, the provision of finance for every good enterprise. Christ had assured them that as they yielded wholly to his will and sought first his kingdom they would not need to be at all anxious about those things that had to be the chief concern of the unbelieving world that they had left to follow him because now they and all these things would come under his own quite special and miraculous care (Cf. Matt. 6:31–33).

We are, of course, justified in taking these words as personal assurance that 'all things work together for good to those who love God' so that we each as individuals might be 'conformed to the image of his Son' (Rom. 8: 28–29). As we follow the way of self-denial and cross-bearing[17] which Christ has marked out as he goes before us and calls us, we will find it also punctuated continually by 'miracles'. Things will happen at times in answer to prayer, at times simply 'out of the blue', as signs that God is near to us, never failing in his watchfulness and purpose. It is his desire that we should be alert to such, kept in wonder, and continually thankful. It would be well if the Church could today continually keep in mind the promise held out to it in the New Testament as the body of Christ, and the warning included in the promise. In too many parts of the world, as it has grown in numbers, in national and international importance in the learning and skills that the world so richly makes possible, it has tended to forget that is is only wise when it is foolish, powerful when it is weak, and that it is Christ alone who is 'the power of God and the wisdom of God' (1 Cor. 1: 18–25). It requires to listen afresh and seriously to the warning of Jeremiah (17:5)

'Thus says the Lord:
Cursed are those who trust in mere mortals
and make the flesh their strength,
whose hearts turn away from the Lord',
and to the contrasting and marvellous promise which immediately follows (v.7),
'Blessed are those who trust in the Lord,
whose trust is the Lord.'

---

[17] See pp.81–83.